CN00863320

COMING TO FAITH

OTHER BOOKS BY BOB LIBBY

The Forgiveness Book
Cowley Publications, 1992
ISBN 1-56101-048-0

Grace Happens
Cowley Publications, 1994
ISBN 1-56101-091-X

COMING TO FAITH

Bob Libby

Authors Choice Press
San Jose New York Lincoln Shanghai

Coming to Faith

All Rights Reserved © 2001 by Bob Libby

No part of this book may be reproduced or transmitted in any form or by
any means, graphic, electronic, or mechanical, including photocopying,
recording, taping, or by any information storage or retrieval system, without
the permission in writing from the publisher.

Authors Choice Press
an imprint of iUniverse, Inc.

For information address:
iUniverse, Inc.
5220 S. 16th St., Suite 200
Lincoln, NE 68512
www.iuniverse.com

Second Revised Edition, 2002

ISBN: 0-595-16403-X

Printed in the United States of America

To all those who have come to Faith in the Living Lord and in so doing
have discovered love, joy and peace in believing.

Contents

Acknowledgements

I am grateful to the dozens of individuals who have entrusted me with their stories.

My thanks go to Dean Guy Lytle, III, the faculty and student body at the School of Theology of the University of the South for their encouragement and invitation to be a "Fellow in Residence" and once again use their research facilities . Dr. Donald Armentrout was particularly helpful in critiquing some of my historical chapters. Conversations with Dr. Robert Hughes gave me fresh insights into the process of individual spiritual formation and John Janeway at the Theological Library was an invaluable resource in my research endeavors.

In London I frequented the British Library and the London institute for Contemporary Christianity. Canon James Rosenthal was kind enough to have me on the Lambert Conference communication team. Andrew Carey of the Church of England Newspaper provided invaluable contacts in the UK . Canon Michael and Jackie Saward not only extended the hospitality of Six Amen Court, but provided helpful insights and encouragement along the way.

Back in Florida, Dr. Elaine Stone gave me support in my enquiry into the C.S. Lewis story. The congregation at St. Christopher's by-the-Sea sent me off to London with a new laptop and Key Biscayne librarian Wayne Powell coached me in doing research on the internet. Mary Tataronis shared her typing skills and The Rev. Dr. Gabriel Sinisi, St. Christopher's new rector and a computer wiz coached me in the final preparation of my floppy disks. Then fellow authors Gini Habeeb and

Irene Erickson encouraged me to keep at it when writer's block appeared to be terminal.

My old friend and former colleague, The Rev. George Young was kind enough to read and critique my manuscript. Last but not least John Ratti, who has been my coach and mentor in my previous endeavors rolled up his sleeves one more time.

In this the Second Revised Edition, I am especially grateful to those friends who had the courage to point out typos and errors in the First Edition. In the old days of publishing, the author provided a manuscript and the typesetters took it from there. This is no longer the case. The writer is both author and typesetter. For some reason my quotation marks were always pointing in the wrong direction. I pray that these and any other errors I may have committed have been corrected. Amen.

Coming to Faith

To be converted, to be regenerated, to receive grace, to experience religion, to gain an assurance, are so many phrases which denote the process, gradual or sudden, by which a self hitherto divided, and consciously wrong, inferior and unhappy becomes unified and consciously right, superior and happy, in consequence of its firmer hold upon religious realities.

William James, *Varieties of Religious Experiences, 1900*

Introduction

There are many terms in use in many traditions and denominations that describe the process by which individuals become Christians. Some talk of being saved; others say they have been born again, accepted Christ, found the Lord, baptized in the Holy Spirit, assured of their salvation. Some associate their becoming Christians with the sacrament, rite, or ordinance of baptism, confirmation, or responding to an altar call, making a profession of faith or joining the church.

I rather like the term "coming to faith' which I first heard from my old friend Canon Michael Saward of St. Paul's Cathedral, London. It seems to include all of the above, implying that becoming a Christian is a journey or a pilgrimage. Besides, the first Christians were known as "people of the way," and that implies a journey or a pilgrimage.

Let me say right at the beginning that I make no claim to being an academic scholar. William James was a psychologist, an academic, and a scholar—and I am not. I am writing from the base of being a parish priest, sometime religious journalist, communicator, and storyteller. I base my claim on my experience in the parish ministry and would argue for the validity of that pastoral experience. We live in the midst of our people. We see them at the super market and the PTA; at the ballpark and on the beach as well as in the hospital, funeral parlor, or at the church door. We visit their homes, see the pictures on their wall, the trophies on their mantles, and we meet their friends and visiting relatives. We know them as friend and neighbor as well as being their pastor, priest, preacher, confidant, advisor, observer, teacher, intercessor, crisis interventionist, spiritual director, program coordinator, fund raiser, parish administrator—or all of the above.

Before I responded to God's call to study for the ministry, I thought, or my family thought, I'm not sure which, that I ought to be an architect. One thing I remember from my experience at Georgia Tech was that the famous Dutch architect Mies Van der Rohe said, "God is in the details." To which I would add, the details of every day life in the community of other Christians is the playing field of the Holy Spirit and provides the data base for this book.

Coming to Faith is my third book to be published and represents a logical extension of the inquiries begun in *The Forgiveness Book* and *Grace Happens.* In going back over the more than forty real life stories in those two volumes, I realized that an act of forgiveness or an experience of grace also became, in many lives, the occasion of conversion, the renewal of faith and/or the strengthening of faith.

In *The Forgiveness Book* I wrote about Gert Behanna in "Why don't you turn it over to God." She was a lady of good breeding, social position, great wealth, and a proper education who had three failed marriages, an attempted suicide, chemical dependency, and alcoholism on her score card. Gert told her own story in a best selling paperback, *The Late Liz.* The defining moment in her life occurred when she was hopelessly hung over and cried out to a friend that she didn't know what to do. The friend, who had taken about as much drunken behavior as she could handle, said, rather sarcastically, "Why don't you turn it over to God?" Gert did and God did. She later reported to all who would listen, " I felt cleansed, welcomed and forgiven." When asked by friends, "My God Gert, what has happened to you?" she would reply, "My God has happened to me."

In "An Unnatural Act," I related the story of, "Big Mike," a hardened criminal and a permanent resident of the Union Correctional Institution near Jacksonville, Florida. He was known by his fellow prison inmates as an angry, arrogant felon who professed to be an atheist and enjoyed ridiculing Christians. Big Mike surprised everyone from the prison chaplain on down by signing up for a weekend retreat, known as *Kairos*, which was conducted by an outside ecumenical team of Episcopalians, Lutherans, and Roman Catholics. When the weekend began, Mike made it perfectly clear that he had come for the cookies and not for the Christianity. He promised to be good and not cause trouble, but declared that it would "take a miracle" for him to become a Christian.

Mike's hard shell developed a few small cracks when he realized that the man serving the Cokes and cookies was the judge who had sentenced him to twenty years. But his defenses collapsed when he heard a Lutheran pastor relate how he had been able to forgive a homeless man whom he had befriended, but who had, in turn, raped and killed his wife. Big Mike could only understand such an act of forgiveness as a miracle and he announced to all who would listen, " There is no way any human being on earth could forgive someone who did what was done to the preacher and his wife. It is absolutely unnatural to forgive in a situation like that. And something that goes against natural law can only be called supernatural. And if that is true, then there must be a God and I thank God for sending Jesus Christ to be my savior."

What I also discovered in writing about forgiveness was that it was but one of many expressions of God's grace. Forgiveness is an important aspect of God's grace for it liberates us from the hurts, mistakes, failures, and sins of the past and it also opens the door to a whole new set of relationships with Christ at the center of our activity.

As a parish priest it has been my practice, when preparing an adult or older adolescent for baptism, to compare the event to cleaning the blackboard at the end of the week. Back in my school days, when a exercise was finished at the end of the day, the teacher or a designated student would erase the blackboard. The results were always incomplete. There was always the chalk dust and if you looked carefully you could detect faint outlines of earlier lessons. But on Friday afternoon, the teacher selected a special student for the coveted task of washing down the blackboard. The lucky guy or girl got to go down to the janitor's office, get a pail of clear water and a clean sponge. Systematically and thoroughly the white markings of a week's classroom experiences were removed and a glistening black surface was left to dry out in preparation for the work of the coming week. I would ask the candidate to imagine that: all of the bad things they had done; all of the mistakes they had made; all of the sins they had committed; were written on the black board. This thought usually sparked a moment of embarrassed discomfort, followed by a sigh of relief when I would then add, "and now imagine the slate being wiped clean with the water of baptism. It's all ready for a new story to be written."

In *Grace Happens* the discovery or experience of God's grace also became the occasion of spiritual re-birth, conversion, or coming to faith. The classical example of this was the story of John Newton author of "Amazing Grace." The words of this popular hymn describe the spiritual journey that began aboard a slave ship on a dark and stormy night when a young man cried for help. The plaque on the wall of St. Mary Woolnoth, London, summarizes the account. Of "John Newton, clerk, once an infidel and a libertine, a servant of slaves in Africa, was by the rich mercy of our Lord and saviour Jesus Christ preserved, restored, pardoned, and appointed to preach the faith he had long labored to destroy."

Most conversions are not as sudden or dramatic, and are often set in motion by a series of unconscious graceful acts or words of witness or encouragement. In "Making a Difference," I reported on a chance meeting in New York with South Africa's Desmond Tutu in which the Archbishop recalled that a turning point in his spiritual journey occurred when he was twelve years of age and confined to a tuberculosis hospital. He was visited almost daily by a tall young English priest in a white cassock and a black hat. What impressed young Desmond was not the frequent visits, but that the priest always tipped his hat to his mother and called her "Ma'am." I had occasion several years later to visit the priest, later to be bishop and archbishop Trevor Huddleston, a legendary opponent of apartheid and by then an old man living in a cluttered apartment at St. James, Picadilly, London. I told him Tutu's story. He smiled, but had no recollection of tipping his hat to Tutu's mother. "I guess that was just something I did instinctively," he said, "I was trained to tip my hat to a lady."

And then there was Sally, "The woman in 208." She was terminally ill with cancer. She was also a constant complainer, a racist, and a bigot and had a most annoying voice. She was estranged from her son who had married a Korean girl and she refused to see their children. A daughter who gave birth to a child out of wedlock was also in disfavor. Sally was a hateful person who became a graceful and a forgiving person before she died. The transformation, as far as I can determine, was prompted by the arrival of a roommate who suggested that they "hold hands, say the Lord's prayer and turn it all over to God."

And so, my fascination with forgiveness and grace, have led me to an exploration of how people have come to faith. Most writers tell me that once a book has begun, it takes on a life of its own. I started my research in the summer of 1998 on the campus of the University of Kent at Canterbury, England. I had been invited to be on the communication staff of the Lambeth Conference. Lambeth is a gathering of Anglican Bishops from around the world at the invitation of the Archbishop of Canterbury. They have been meeting for every ten years since 1868. It's called the Lambeth Conference because they used to meet at Lambeth Palace, the London residence of the Archbishop. It was sort of a big six week house party, sort of an old boy's club and, except for the Americans, something of an Oxford and Cambridge reunion. Lambeth has not only outgrown its British-ness, its old school tie ambiance, but its all maleness as well . There were 750 bishops invited to the 1998 gathering. The majority were non-British and non-Caucasian, and eleven were not "boys" at all! Eleven women in purple cassocks came from Canada, New Zealand, and the United States. I squeezed in as many visits with prelates as I could, but their busy 12 hour a day schedules of meetings and activities plus my daily assignments as a reporter for the Lambeth Daily newspaper limited the occasions for interviews just with bishops. Along with the folks in purple robes was a small army of young people wearing yellow T-shirts. They were volunteers from around the world who were known as "stewards." They served as pages, runners, helpers, and what New Yorkers would call "schleppers." They had some interesting stories to tell and broadened the generational base of my inquiry.

When Lambeth was over after three intensive weeks, my wife and I had the good fortune to have the use of Michael and Jackie Saward's townhouse in Amen Court near St. Paul's Cathedral, London, where Michael is a senior canon. The Saward's went "on holiday" while the Libbys had the run of the place. I did research at the British Library and the London Institute of Contemporary Christianity during the day while Lynne, a professional artist, haunted the art museums and galleries. At night we did the West End theaters and concert halls. The time in London took my search into several new avenues of religious experience. Both Terry Waite, the former hostage, and Susan Howatch, the author, were kind enough to spend an afternoon at Amen court. Visiting some of the livelier London churches put us in touch with some unique laypeople, who also had interesting stories to tell. A chance encounter at the London Institute with folks who were returning from a C.S. Lewis seminar at Oxford led me to a meaningful transatlantic telephone and E-mail correspondence with Doug Gresham, son of Joy Davidman Lewis and the stepson of C. S. Lewis. One person led to another. The encounter with Joy Davidman's conversion and her husband's faith journey took me across the border into the realm of historical figures. On an afternoon walk around St. Paul's Cathedral, I found a statue of John Wesley hiding in the bushes. A friendly tourist, observing my interest in the figure of Methodism's founder offered, "You know the place where he had his Aldersgate experience is only a few blocks north of here." An interview with Eileen Carey, wife of the Archbishop of Canterbury, opened the door to the life and ministry of Billy Graham. Dr. Graham's first British crusade had a profound effect on Eileen's life as it did on the lives of millions of people around the world. Then there was the retired Roman Catholic priest from Santa Fe, New Mexico, who shared chaplain duties with me on a QE2 Christmas cruise. Fr. Tom Mc Laughlin had earned his Ph.D. at the Pontifical College in Rome. The subject of his thesis was Augustine of Hippo and Anselm of Milan. The daily reading of the venerable Episcopal publication, *Forward Day by Day,* introduced me to Bo Cox, a convicted murderer and new Christian at an Oklahoma State Prison. Then the tragic massacre at the Columbine High School in Littleton, Colorado brought the heroic figure of Cassie Bernall into the collection.

And so my community in Christ grew. I started with what I hoped would be a cross section of Anglican bishops and their spirituality and little by little my book demanded that we broaden the scope and take on intergenerational, historical, and ecumenical dimensions.

I write from my base as an Episcopal pastor and priest and as a religious communicator and journalist. What I am trying to do is describe, as best I can, the defining moment or process which brought individuals into a conscious relationship with the living God through his son Jesus Christ. In St. Paul's journey, for instance, there was an instantaneous transformation, in the case of C. S. Lewis there was gradual turning to the light. For some, like Augustine of Hippo, Thomas Merton, and Susan Howatch there was a long intellectual struggle before coming to faith. In others, like the Iranian woman, Jahleh Mac Donald, the movement to faith was more emotional and mystical. In other stories, like those of Michael Saward of London, Bishop Francis of the Sudan, and Louis Tsui of Hong Kong there was a close encounter with death at an early age which made them wrestle with the very personal questions, "Why am I here? If my life was spared by God, was it spared for a purpose?" In some cases the call to faith and the call to ministry occurred at the same time. Lucy Winkett, the first woman priest to serve on the staff of St. Paul's, Cathedral, London, experienced both a renewal of her faith and a call to priesthood at the same time. This by the way, is very Biblical. Most of the great conversion stories in the Old Testament are about call to special ministry. This certainly was the case with Abraham (Genesis 12:1-3), Moses (Exodus 3:1-15), Samuel (1 Samuel 3:1-21), David (1 Samuel 16:1-13), Isaiah (Isaiah 6:1-8) and Jeremiah (Jeremiah 1:4-10).

In addition my observation is that the intellectual struggle of theism versus atheism, between is there a God or is there no God, is a relatively modern phenomenon. In spite of the Psalmist's note, "The fool has said in his heart, there is no God," (Psalm 14:1), the issue in the Hebrew Bible is not is there a God? The issue is, rather, does God care about us and does God have the power to help us? What does he demand of us? And then a bit later on, is the God of Abraham, Isaac, and Jacob, truly universal; is God in fact the creator and king of the universe. When we move into the New Testament, the pivotal issue has to do with the resurrection of Jesus, quickly followed by "was he the promised messiah? Did his death on the cross establish a new relationship with God? Was the gift of the Holy Spirit and the church an extension of his ministry? Was Jesus in fact Savior of the world and Lord of all life? Had Jesus in fact established a new Covenant for all humanity?"

Paul's conversion was not a conversion to God. He already believed that there was a Supreme Being. Paul's God was the God of the Torah, of the patriarchs and the prophets. Paul was zealous in his faith. He looked for the redemption of Israel with the coming of the promised messiah. As a Pharisee, he had a very clear idea of how the messiah was going to behave. Paul's Damascus Road experience (Acts 9:1-19; 22:5-16; and 26:12-18) was not a conversion to God, but a complete 180 degree turn around to that fact Jesus was the promised Messiah, that he had been crucified, and that God had raised him from the dead. In the case of

Philip's baptism of the Ethiopian diplomat, the issue was not, "is there a God?" but "is Jesus the promised Messiah." When the Ethiopian was convinced from scripture that this was the case, he asked to be baptized. (Acts 8: 26-40). Simon Peter's journey, along with the other apostles, began with Jesus' invitation, "Follow me." (Matthew 4:18-22, Mark 1:16-20, Luke 5:2-11, John 1:35-42) A defining moment came with Peter's confession: "You are the Christ."(Matthew 16:13-20;Mark 8:27-29;Luke 9:18-20). But an even more significant moment was the resurrection appearance in Galilee, where the apostle who had denied his Lord three times was forgiven and commissioned to "Feed my Sheep." (John 21:15-19). The experience of the Holy Spirit on Pentecost (Acts 2:1-47) not only confirmed the original apostles and disciples in the reality of Jesus' resurrection, but also empowered them for ministry and, along with Peter's preaching, attracted many converts from among the Jewish observers. Peter declared that God had raised Jesus from the dead. That Jesus was the fulfillment of the ancient prophesies. And he challenged them to "repent and be baptized every one of you in the name of Jesus Christ so that your sins may be forgiven; and you will receive the gift of the Holy Spirit. For the promise is for you and your children, and for all who are far away, everyone whom the Lord calls to him." (Acts 2:37-39) It was reported that the reaction was rather overwhelming and that "about 3,000" responded. The Pentecost account concludes with the observation that this was the beginning, not the end, and that, "They continued in the apostles teaching and fellowship, in the breaking of bread and the prayers." (Acts 2:42).

Then, in the account of the Roman officer, Cornelius (Acts 10: 1-48) it is noted that Christ's ministry and the gift of the Holy Spirit was not only for Jews, but gentiles as well. Cornelius was one of many gentiles, known as "God Fearers," who had been attracted to the high ethical teachings and monotheism of the synagogue. While it took an act of God to overcome some of Peter's hang ups about trafficking with non-Jews, Peter witnessed to the resurrection and said of Jesus, "He is the

xxiv / Coming to Faith

one ordained by God as judge of the living and the dead. All the prophets testify about him that everyone who believes in him receives forgiveness of sins through his name." During Peter's speech, the Holy Spirit fell upon all who heard the word, both circumcised and uncircumcised, and then Peter decided that baptism could not be withheld from those who had, "received the Holy Spirit just as we have." And so the stage was set for the apostles to go out into the world with a simple invitation. Paul, writing to the Christians in the capital of the empire, put it this way, "if you confess with your lips that Jesus is Lord and that God raised him from the dead, you will be saved."

I believe that's about all the scriptural background that we need at this point. When you turn the page you will meet real people with true experiences of coming to faith. Along with each story there will be a selection from scripture, either chosen by the subject, or appropriate to their faith journey. In the tradition established in my earlier books I have included a few observations and or questions for reflection and then the words of a hymn or spiritual song. In earlier books, I concluded with an appropriate prayer, but this time each chapter ends with a hymn. The reason is not that I've run out of prayers or that this book doesn't have a prayer, but the discovery of the tremendous influence hymns have had in the lives of the people in this book.

Well, there it is: turn the page and begin, or continue, your own journey during which you will meet some fellow pilgrims who have come to faith in Jesus and acknowledged him as Lord.

Chapter One

For God Alone My Soul In Silence Waits

Thomas Merton

It seems appropriate to begin this book with Thomas Merton because he and I had our own beginnings in the same village on Long Island. His grandfather and mine had both been pioneers in that north shore community created by the extension of the Long Island Railroad from Flushing to Port Washington. Before the railroad got to Douglaston, the area had been the domain of the Douglas family, whose manor house presided over a small peninsula, which had been taken by force from the original Native American occupants. The bay yielded an abundance of shell fish that had been reshaped into wampum, making it the Native American financial center of Long Island. Today the old Douglas home is the Douglaston Club and from the top floor you can see Long Island Sound, the Whitestone and Throgs' Neck Bridges; planes taking off and landing at LaGuardia Airport, and the skyline of Manhattan.

Merton wrote about the commuter train breaking out of the urban landscape of Bayside and gliding across the meadow lands to Douglaston and seeing the "pale, soft haze of summer beginning to hang over the bay, and count the boats that had been set afloat again after the winter, and were riding jauntily at their moorings off the end of the little dock." I used to swim off that dock and so did Merton. As a little boy, Thomas accompanied his father, who was a sometime organist, to Zion Episcopal Church. The white frame building, built around 1820, sat on the highest hill in town and was surrounded by an even more ancient cemetery. As a little boy I attended that same church with my grandfather, who was an usher and on the vestry. The Zion churchyard now contains the bodies of both my parents, all four of my grandparents, and assorted aunts, uncles, and cousins. Between Douglaston and Little Neck, the next stop on the railroad, there was a deep ravine and swampy no man's land overgrown with sawgrass and sumac trees, alive with mosquitoes. This area was a natural battlefield for the young boys of both communities. The folks in Douglaston were mostly members of the Community Church or the Episcopal Church. The Little Neck kids in those days were mostly Polish and many of them attended St. Anastasia's Roman Catholic Church. Although Tom was fifteen years my senior, my generation built our secret huts in the same bushes and fought over the same turf his generation had battled over.

Imagine the excitement in Douglaston when Thomas Merton's *Seven Story Mountain* was published in 1948 and quickly became a national bestseller. Books and Things, the little shop by the railroad station received a fresh shipment from Harcourt Brace each week, but still couldn't keep up with the demand. The stir went way beyond the local boy has written a book syndrome. Merton, at 33, told the story of the spiritual journey that had taken him into the Roman Catholic Church and, ultimately, into a monastery of the Order of Cistercians of the Strict Observance, commonly known as Trappists. In addition to the vows of poverty, chastity and obedience, the Trappists observed a life of hard manual labor, frequent fasting, and total silence, except when addressed by a superior or involved in worship with other members of the community. The discipline was designed to encourage contemplation. Trappists took pride in the fact that theirs was often called "the hardest life to be found in the church."

In chronicling his own spiritual journey into the contemplative life, Merton had written of his profound disappointment with the theological convictions of the Rev. Dr. Lester Leak Riley, the rector of Zion-on-the Hill, Douglaston. Merton wrote that Riley, "did not know his vocation and did not know what he was supposed to be." My mother was among those who thought that the book was right on target, recalling a Good Friday sermon, where Riley had focused on Socrates drinking the hemlock, but made nary a mention of Jesus and the cross. Others thought Merton had taken a cheap and unkind shot, especially since Dr. Riley was dead and couldn't defend himself. Among those objecting was Riley's widow, who was, by then, teaching English at Smith College. Mrs. Riley made a trip to Merton's monastery, Our Lady of Gethsemani Trappist Monastery in Kentucky. The word around Douglaston was that she had pleaded with Merton to retract or at least soften his comments about her husband in future editions of his book. But Merton, the story went, simply listened politely to her and, invoking the Trappist rule of silence, shrugged his shoulders, made the sign of the cross, and returned to his cell.

Fifty years later, on one of my own retreats at the Trappist Monastery of the Holy Ghost, Conyers, Georgia, I discovered that Thomas Merton was still a controversial figure, even among the monks. Some considered the famous writer an embarrassment to the order. While the monastery bookstore was doing a brisk business in Merton books, tapes and memorabilia, back in the cloister they spoke of their personal disappointment in Merton. In the last volume of his journal, which had only recently been published, Merton revealed that he had fallen deeply in love and had an affair with a student nurse who attended him when he had been hospitalized in Louisville. However, one monk admitted that Merton's *Seven Story Mountain* had indeed led him into the order. "I read the book," said Fr. Bob, the Trappist in question, " and I knew that I wanted to be a Trappist monk. I told my father, who wanted me to go into the family business, and he got drunk!" Fr. Bob had also come to have reservations about Merton, but as a spiritual director and confessor he understood only too well the frailty and weakness of all human beings, be they bishops, monks, or just plain working folk. Fr. Bob was glad that Merton ended the affair and returned to his monastic vows.

Others among the Trappists expressed concerns that penetrated deeply into the very soul of the man. "He found it impossible to live the simple life of a Trappist," I was told by one veteran of more than 40 years in the order. "He became a contemplative writer-in-residence at the monastery—a monastic sport, a monastic mutant whose activity had a viral effect on Trappist monastic life."

All of which seem to be saying that Merton was a very complex person torn between the need for solitude and the need for an audience; the need for silence and the demand for applause.

As a child Merton never stayed in one place very long. He was born in Padres, France, of American and New Zealand parents. His father, an artist, traveled widely in search of the perfect subject matter. This took young Tom to Bermuda, France, and England with boarding schools along the way. The only stable place in his life was Douglaston.

Tom's spiritual development did not follow a set course either. As an infant he had been christened, but he did not think that there was, "much power in the water." He speculated that his parents' highest hopes were that he would grow up to be "a quiet Deist and never be perverted by superstition." When he was four, his parents moved to Flushing, which was only five miles via Northern Boulevard, from his mother's parents, called Pop and Bonnemaman, in Douglaston. His father painted pictures, but earned a meager living as a gardener and handy man. From his bedroom Thomas could hear the bells of St. George's, Flushing's old Episcopal Church, and when the bells rang, the birds began to sing. He remembered asking, "Father, all the birds are in the church, why can't we go there, too?" From time to time his mother slipped off to the venerable Quaker Meeting House on Bowne Street in Flushing, but she always went alone. Somewhere during this period Bonnemaman taught Tom to say the Lord's Prayer, but there was no provision for any formal Christian education. Merton's father was also a musician and earned extra cash playing the piano at the movie house on Bell Boulevard in Bayside. Then on Sunday he played the organ at

Zion Church in Douglaston. Little Thomas finally got to go to church as well as ride the trolley car with his father. He was fascinated by the symbolism of an anchor in one of the stained glass windows. Thomas was interested in anything to do with boats and ships. He had already crossed the Atlantic once and he constantly drew pictures of ocean liners with many smoke stacks, hovering sea gulls, and large waves. For his father, Zion Church was a job. For Thomas it was a pleasant experience. Even at age six he came out of church with, "the comfortable and satisfied feeling that something had been done that needed to be done." He also paid one visit to the old Quaker Meeting House in Flushing to see Dan Beard, one of the founders of the Boy Scouts. Thomas had two questions on his mind: did Mr. Beard have a beard? and what was the Holy Spirit going to move the people to say or do? Beard, in fact, did have a beard, but the activities of the Holy Spirit were not that easily recognized. Technically, Pop and Bonnemaman were members of Zion Church. They put cash in the little offering envelopes the church provided and sent them in, but they never attended. Thomas recalls that Pop's "favorite place of worship was the Capitol Theater in New York."

When he was six, Tom Merton's mother died. He had only been vaguely aware of the fact that she was ill, but one day he was given a hand written letter from his mother informing him that she was dying and that he would not see her again. A great burden and gloom descended on the little boy.

Sadly, it never occurred to him to pray. When the end came, he rode in a hired car to the hospital with his father, grandparents, and an uncle. He stayed in the car for what seemed like a very long time. When the family returned to the car, no one told him what had happened, but he knew. They rode in silence back to Douglaston. He remembers his father going off by himself to weep. Several days later, the same limousine took the family to the crematorium. There was no rite, ceremony, or funeral. A relative waited in the car with him. It was twenty years later that he found that he could pray for his mother.

Merton accompanied his father on painting excursions to Cape Cod and then to Bermuda. At the end of these trips, he was deposited back in Douglaston. His father, following a successful show and sale of his paintings in New York, took off for France and North Africa. It was during the formative years between six and nine that Thomas experienced the predominately White Anglo Saxon Protestant (WASP) ethos of Long Island's North Shore in those days. To be Christian meant that you were a nice person with decent manners and that you weren't Jewish. To be Protestant meant that you weren't a Roman Catholic. In Pop's mind Catholicism and Tammany Hall were synonymous. Tammany was corrupt and Catholicism was superstitious. Thomas did attend Sunday school with a friend, but found it a bore. He preferred to wander off on Sunday morning and play in the woods. He remembered at this time, " becoming more and more adverse to the thought of any religion." He does remember praying for his father when a letter arrived saying that he was seriously ill and was not expected to live. "It was probably," he later wrote, "only one of those blind instinctive moments of nature that will come to anyone, even an atheist in a time of crisis." Merton's father did not die and returned to New York in 1924, wearing a beard, and announced that he planned to take his eldest son off to Europe on his next painting venture. Thomas wasn't all that pleased. He was almost ten and had begun to settle in. He had friends; they rowed their boats and swam in the bay. They were all planning to be Boy Scouts. But off to France Thomas went.

In his father's company, he received the "only really valuable religious and moral training he ever got as a child." In the course of spontaneous daily conversation, his father spoke of Peter's denial of Christ in such a way that Tom felt what Peter must have felt. Likewise, his father passed on an understanding of Christ's command to love one's enemies, not for the enemies' sake, or for God's sake, but for one's own sake. "It was

St. Augustine's argument," noted Merton, "that when envy and hatred try to pierce our neighbor with a sword, then the blade can not reach him unless it first passes through our own body. I suppose Father had never read any of St. Augustine, but he would have liked him."

While in France, Thomas and his father boarded with the Privat family in Murat. The Privats were a loving Roman Catholic couple who listened patiently to the American lad's declarations of "non-faith" and conveyed to him their deep concern over his non-belief. "Who knows," he wrote, "how much I owe to those two wonderful people? It is to me a matter of moral certitude that I owe many graces to their prayers and perhaps ultimately, the grace of my conversion and even my religious vocation."

About the time that Thomas was getting used to growing up as a Frenchman, he and his father crossed the channel to England. It was 1928; he was approaching fourteen and he thought he might like to be a novelist. This was interpreted by the headmistress of his new English school as Tom wanting to be a "dilettante like his father."

In the succession of English boarding schools he attended, there was the experience of school chapel and the weekly trek to the local parish church. "We all sat in rows in our black Eton jackets and our snow white Eton collars choking us up to the chin, and bent our well brushed and combed heads over the pages of our hymnals. At last I was really going to church." On Sunday evenings there was a hymn sing and study of Bunyan's *Pilgrim's Progress.* In the dormitory, Merton recalls seeing other boys kneel at the side of their beds and pray and in the refectory, there was grace before meals. "Thus at the time when I most needed it, I did acquire a little natural faith and found many occasions of praying and lifting up my mind to God." He found an inner peace during those early adolescent years, which he later referred to as his "religious phase."

That phase came to an abrupt end when Merton's father died of a brain tumor. Summoned to his father's bedside, Thomas heard his father say, "Pray to God to make me well." He prayed.

After Merton's father died, depression and cynicism set in.

In a year that Thomas described as a "Harrowing of Hell," his school masters introduced him to the philosophy of Descartes. Thomas was not convinced that God could exist simply because Descartes imagined such a thing. And then there was the school chaplain, who in an effort to be modern and up to date suggested that what Paul meant by *charity* in I Corinthians 13, was really nothing more, or less, than the attributes of a British gentleman. Certainly, a person dedicated to good sportsmanship—as in "A gentleman is patient. A gentleman is kind. He does not envy. A gentleman does not boast. He is not proud or rude etc." It was a clever homiletical gimmick, but Merton's grief and his needs were deep. He would have none of it.

Pop and Bonnemaman sailed over from the States to be of comfort and to assure him of a sizable inheritance that would be available to complete his education. There was also a godfather who stepped into the parental void. But at age fifteen Thomas was determined to nurse his bitterness and resentment. The little bit of religion he had begun to acquire died with his father. There simply was no room in his life for God. He described his own soul as "empty, dead, a vacuum." He fancied himself a communist, although he hardly knew what a communist might believe or be. His bookshelf now contained D. H. Lawrence and he professed belief, "in the beautiful myth of having a good time as long as it does not hurt someone else."

The downward spiral of his life came to a temporary halt when he visited Rome during a school holiday. It was the early Christian mosaics in the ancient city that helped him understand for the first time who Christ was. He wanted to know more and he began to read the Gospels for the first time. It was also in Rome that he had a mystical experience.

I was in my room. It was night. The light was on. Suddenly it seemed to me that Father, who had now been dead for more than a year was there with me. The sense of his presence was as vivid and as real and as startling as if he had touched my arm or spoken to me. The whole thing passed in a flash, instantly I was overwhelmed with a sudden and profound insight into the misery and corruption of my own soul, and I was pierced deeply with a light that filled me with horror at what I saw, and my whole being rose up in revolt against what was within me, and my soul desired escape and liberation and freedom from all this with an intensity and an urgency unlike anything I had ever known before.

And now I think for the first time in my whole life I really began to pray.

The experience was baptized with a river of tears. From then on when he visited a church, he would kneel down and pray, beginning with the only prayer that he had ever been taught," Our Father......"

One of the sanctuaries he visited in Rome was up in the hills at the Monastery of Tre Fontane. The monastery was occupied by Trappists. As young Merton, now age sixteen, re-boarded the rickety tourist bus, he wondered what it would be like to be a Trappist monk.

Two weeks and an ocean voyage later, he was back in his grandparents' home in Douglaston. He read his Bible daily, but privately. He said his prayers, but he did not kneel at the side of his bed lest someone see him and make fun of his behavior. He had looked forward to attending Zion Church, but he found nothing there to reinforce his new experience. He thought he might go to a Quaker meeting. The idea of silence and waiting for the inspiration of the Holy Spirit intrigued him, but that too was a disappointment. He tried reading William Penn, but found him "about as supernatural as a Montgomery Ward catalogue." He read a tract or two from the Mormons, but found them unconvincing and uninspiring. By the time he was eighteen, Merton had lost most of his interest in religion. Besides, he had made friends in Manhattan and the "bigness, and gaudiness and noisiness and frank animality and vulgarity of this

American paganism" began to draw him in. He would have been happy to stay in New York, but an ocean liner, at Pop's direction, took him back to England to prepare for a career in the British diplomatic corps. The year was 1933.

At Cambridge he plunged into the great "isms" of the twentieth century. He read Freud and Jung and Adler and was warned of the dangers of sexual repression. Karl Marx instructed him in the evils of capitalism. But diplomacy was not for him. He returned to New York, in Columbia University, and was known in the local Communist Party as Frank Swift. It was a double life, living with Pop and Bonnemaman in capitalist Douglaston and joining party demonstrations and parades in Manhattan chanting, "Pie in the sky when you die, it's a lie." This all came to an end when he was 21 and his grandparents died within nine months of each other. He prayed for the first time in more than four years.

The deaths were followed by Merton's emotional collapse with a panic attack while riding the Long Island Railroad into the city. He managed to find a room at the Pennsylvania Hotel. His head was pounding and spinning, his stomach was churning, and his heart thumping. He was gripped with fear and considered throwing himself out the window, but called for the house physician instead. He never did find out what had happened. He guessed that he had a nervous breakdown. His own self image was shattered. He had seen himself as a great success at Columbia: track star, editor of the yearbook, cartoonist, party person, jazz piano player, intellectual. He had taken pride in his reputation as "a noisy bastard." But inside, spiritually, emotionally, he was "bleeding to death."

The railroad incident for Merton also marked a great divide which would eventually separate him from Douglaston, the non-religious WASP culture that it represented, and his own childhood.

In spite of the very secular bent his intellectual life had taken, there were seeds from a different source which had been planted along the way. In boarding school he had been captivated by the mystical art and writings of William Blake. Someone had slipped him a copy of the poetry of Fr. Gerald Manley Hopkins, the Jesuit poet. And at Cambridge he had taken a course in Dante's *Divine Comedy*. Little by little, the seeds began to germinate. A defining moment occurred in February, 1937. Walking past the window of Scribner's Bookstore on Fifth Avenue, he spotted copies of *The Spirit of Medieval Philosophy* by Etienne Gilson. At first he was offended by the official imprimatur of the Roman Catholic Church he found inside. But, nonetheless he bought the book and he read it and found "a notion of God that was at the same time deep, precise, simple and accurate and, what is more, charged with implications which I could not even begin to appreciate." Gilson also introduced Thomas to the concept of *asetas*. It is the idea that God is pure existence-being itself. It was a basic idea that had been around for a long time. It had gotten Moses' attention in the burning bush incident when Moses heard YHWH's voice say, "I am Who I am!" or "I will be Who I will be."(Exodus 3:14} It had certainly gotten Moses' attention and now it had grabbed Merton. The intellectual encounter reawakened in Thomas a thirst for prayer, for the Bible, for faith, and for worship. He put aside his old feelings and walked up the long driveway to Zion-on-the-Hill. Alas, Dr. Riley, true to form, talked about modern literature and politics and not about God.

Back in Manhattan, Thomas reflected that, "God brought me and a half dozen others together at Columbia." One was Professor Mark Van Doren. Merton enrolled in his course on Shakespeare quite by accident. Van Doren was excited about his subject and found in the Bard of Avon a creative presenter of the great issues of human existence: life, death, time, love, sorrow, fear, wisdom, suffering, and eternity. Van Doren's classes were so exciting that his pupil was even willing to overcome his anxieties and panic attacks and attempt the thirty minute ride on the LIRR to attend class.

Then there was Bramachari, something of an itinerate Hindu monk and mystic, who urged Merton to read Augustine's *Confessions* and Thomas a Kempis' *Imitation of Christ*. He also encouraged Thomas in the direction of the Roman Catholic Church with the off comment that he felt that that was the only church in which people were really praying.

Merton chose William Blake as the subject of his masters thesis. He read Jacques Maritain's *Art and Scholasticism* in a course on Thomas Aquinas taught by a Jesuit. Sy Freegood, a fellow student and a philosophy major, helped him bat ideas back and forth over a bottle of scotch into the early morning hours. Reading Aldous Huxley's *Ends and Means* opened the door to asceticism and mysticism. Thomas Merton was ripe for a change.

Pop's old home in Douglaston held him to a past that he was now rejecting. His parents were dead. Pop and Bonnemaman were dead. John Paul, Merton's younger brother, had gone off to Cornell. There was nothing left in Douglaston for Thomas. And besides there was that dreaded daily ride on the Long Island Railroad. On a rainy day in June of 1938, as war clouds were gathering over Europe, Thomas hired a local taxi and moved his belongings to a rooming house on 114th Street.

Then one weekend in August, he canceled his plans with a young lady on Long Island. He was overwhelmed by what he called "a sweet, strong, gentle clean urge which said, 'Go to Mass!'" He found Corpus Christi Church hidden behind Columbia Teacher's College on 121st Street. A young priest talked with conviction about the incarnation—Christ being God's word that had been made flesh. Thomas was impressed and he bounced down Broadway that Sunday. He was at peace, content with life, and felt he was walking in a new world. He also noted that, "It was the first time I had ever really spent a sober Sunday in New York."

Back on the campus he had moved from being a communist and an atheist to one who accepted the full range of possibilities for religious experience. He not only accepted the possibility, but began to desire it.

He considered enrolling in the (Protestant) Union Theological Seminary, but nothing in their catalogue caught his fancy. His life was becoming more and more under the influence of Roman Catholic teaching. Then one day:

> *I took up the book about Gerald Manley Hopkins. The chapter told of Hopkins at Balliol, at Oxford. He was thinking of becoming a Catholic. He was writing letters to Cardinal Newman ….All of a sudden, something began to stir within me, something began to push me, to prompt me. It was a movement that spoke like a voice. "What are you waiting for?" it said. "Why are you sitting here? Why do you still hesitate? You know what you ought to do? Why don't you do it?"*
>
> *I stirred in the chair, I lit a cigarette, I looked out the window at the rain, I tried to shut the voice up. "Don't act on impulses," I thought. "This is crazy. This is not rational. Read your book." Hopkins was writing to Newman, at Birmingham, about his indecision. "What are you waiting for?" said the voice within me again. "Why are you sitting there? It is useless to hesitate any longer. Why don't you get up and go?"*

Thomas Merton put down his book; put on his raincoat and hurried up Broadway to Corpus Christi Church and announced, " Father, I want to become a Catholic."

On November 16, 1938, the priest poured water on Thomas' head and said, "If thou be not already baptized, I baptize thee in the name of the Father, and of the Son and of the Holy Ghost."

Scripture

For God alone my soul in silence waits;
  From him comes my salvation.

Psalm 62:1
1979 Book of Common Prayer

Reflection

When I first read *The Seven Story Mountain* I was in college and Merton's break with what he perceived to be the culture and beliefs of Douglaston gave me the courage to venture out on my own. Two decades later, when I was an Episcopal priest and moved back to New York as a staff member at our national headquarters, I discovered that there was far more faith in the little village of Douglaston than I had imagined. Part of growing up as a Christian entails letting go of the past so that the Gospel can be discovered afresh.

My second observation is that God is a stalker. Merton didn't find God. God, finally after a number of narrow escapes caught Thomas Merton. This will be a recurring theme in this small volume. In the famous poem *The Hound of Heaven* God is pictured as the aggressor. As Merton reflected on his own coming to faith, he noted that God's grace was at work in his life long before he was aware of it. The early Christians understood this to be God's prevenient grace, meaning that God's love and care was out there, way ahead of us, preparing for the day when we would respond. From the time of Thomas' first baptism, from the time the birds sang and the bells rang, from the time his Bonnemaman taught him the Lord's Prayer, the Lord was calling Thomas. While it is embarrassing to see how many times the Episcopal Church fell short, it is also encouraging to discover that God never gives up on us.

There is also, running through Merton's journey, the need for the older generation to be pro-active in the spiritual development of the younger generation. "If your child asks for bread will you give him a stone?" (Matthew 7:9) It's fashionable in some circles to say, "I won't impose anything on my children, I'll let him/her make up their own mind etc." HA! I believe that comes under the heading of child neglect.

Hymn

Before the ending of the day,
Creator of the world we pray;
That, with thy wonted favor, thou,
Wouldst be our guard and keeper now.

From all ill dreams defend our sight,
From fears and terrors of the night;
Withhold from us our ghostly foe,
That spot of sin we may not know.

O Father, that we ask be done,
Through Jesus Christ thine only son,
Who, with the Holy Ghost and Thee,
Doth live and reign eternally. Amen

6th century Latin plainsong
Often sung at Compline

Chapter Two

He Keeps Our Tears In A Bottle

Bo Cox

It sat on the kitchen table and it was part of grandfather's morning ritual in Douglaston. He would pick up the little booklet, read a page, stare out the window, put a coin in a metal can and then, finally, pour himself a cup of coffee. We were all under a strict rule of silence until he lifted his cup a second time and wished everybody a "good morning." Sometimes "everybody" was just me. My grandmother seldom appeared in the kitchen until grandfather had left for the train station. What was always present was a copy of *Forward Day By Day*, a small pocket sized pamphlet which had a daily Bible verse followed by a devotional thought or two for the day. It is similar to *The Upper Room* produced by the United Methodist Church and a dozen other daily devotional booklets from a variety of religious traditions. The tin can filled with coins was "for the missionaries" and provided an essential chunk of grandfather's spirituality. Once in a while he would read me a line or two, but it was essentially a private matter.

When I went off to college he sent me my own copy, which daily or to be perfectly honest, I should say "almost" day by day has provided a base for my own devotional life. *Forward Day by Day* invites a variety of writers, male and female, clerical and lay, young and old, and of course ethnically diverse to write a month's worth of meditations. Sometimes the less than 100 word reflections are very meaningful, even profound. Sometimes we don't connect at all. But at its worst it's only a short read, and there's the satisfaction, which I'm sure my grandfather felt from time to time, of having done one's spiritual duty in spite of the discomfort involved.

It was in the autumn of 1995 that I discovered a particularly sensitive writer. Commenting on the return of the Prodigal Son in Luke 15, he wrote, "I know a man who can relate to this story…me."

The author identified himself only as "an incarcerated prisoner." I wrote to Forward Publications to find out more. My inquiry started a correspondence via US Mail and then E-mail which at this writing has spanned more than five years. As it turned out, I was one of more than 600 persons who wanted to know more about the writer. The meditations came from the pen of Bo Cox, an inmate in an Oklahoma State prison.

Ironically Bo had grown up close to a state prison. Many times he had driven by the chain gangs and his father had pointed out the "thieves, rogues, and adulterers," clad in their blue prison shirts, hoeing weeds and picking up trash. As a young lad Bo saw the prisoners as a different kind of species. Those were the bad people. Bo was one of the good people. He was a Boy Scout. He was even an acolyte, "feeling a bit priestly " as he stood before the altar with a towel on his arm "ready to serve." Even though Bo was undersized, he made the football team when he was a freshman. He was smart, too, and finished his freshman year with a 4.0 average. Everybody, Coach Mayer, Father Bill, his teachers, parents, and grandparents all agreed that he has a great future. He was an All American Boy. But then, at age 15, he started experimenting with drugs. At graduation he marched into the school auditorium with a gold braid on the shoulder of his gown indicating that he was in the top 20% of his class. But his chemical addictions began to take their toll on his ability to study. By the time he was 20, Bo had been expelled from three colleges. By age 23, he had received a life sentence for murder. The dead man's name was Bart, who was 18 when Bo killed him in a drunken brawl. The driving force was not so much anger or hatred, but fear. "I was scared of getting beaten up," said Bo, "and getting ridiculed for that or its more shameful alternative, backing down."

When Bo was awaiting trial in the county jail, he was visited by a well meaning preacher who told him that God would get him out of prison if he believed certain things and prayed a certain way. At that point Bo was ready to try anything. But it didn't work. The sentence handed down was as severe as possible. Bo blamed himself and was angry with God.

When I first made contact with Bo, he was living in an 8'x10' cinder block cell that he shared with another prisoner. Their home was equipped with bunk beds, a 13 inch color TV, a wash basin, and a toilet without a seat. In the prison corridor there were the sounds of jingling keys, and steel doors opening and slamming shut. There were also the noises of arguments and the hacking coughs of terminal smokers down the hall. Sometimes noise came in from a fight in the yard outside. On weekends when visitors are allowed, Bo woke up to the rhythm of children playing and laughing, thumping basketballs, and rattling the chains of the play yard swings. So goes the life of Oklahoma prisoner #150656. When he's not in Cell A2-120, Bo works as an orderly in the prison's mental health unit, for which he receives an allowance of $27.00 a month.

A major person in Bo's life was his grandfather, a recovering alcoholic who never gave up on him and loved him even when he couldn't love him back. While prison cut Bo off from the outside world, it didn't separate him from a readily available drug supply. His dependency continued. His grandfather urged him to seek the help of Alcoholics Anonymous. After four years of incarceration, Bo observed a former drug user standing in the canteen line. "He was the calm in a storm, a candle in the dark." The serenity of that notorious figure haunted Bo for several days. Then on April 6, 1990, Bo put down his drugs, walked into the prison AA meeting and took the first of twelve steps. He admitted that he was powerless over his addiction and that his life was unmanageable. He asked for help and "drew his first sober breath in over 12 years.

Along with the sobriety came the rediscovery of feelings. Since his mid teens he had done his level best to stay loaded. "It seemed that there was this great emotion hiding right under the surface and if I didn't stay chemically contained, it would begin to slip up on me and overwhelm me," he wrote.

But there were raw emotions that came right along with the sobriety. The prison chapter of AA helped, but Christmas was coming and that's a difficult time. Every time Bo heard a Christmas carol or watched a holiday program on TV, he had to fight back the tears. "The closer it got to Christmas, the more I felt like I was about to come apart at the seams."

Barely able to keep his emotions under control, Bo stayed in his cell until some friends came by his cell to get him to go to an AA meeting. It was not an easy sell. Bo didn't want to go. Make that, Bo was afraid to go! In prison you don't expose your feelings and above all you don't lose your cool.

But there he was sitting in an AA meeting on Christmas night. The other people there, all recovering alcoholics, talked about their own emerging spirituality and their memories and feelings of Christmases past . Bo sat and listened. "Every few minutes" he recalls, "that wave of emotion would try to rush in and overtake me and I'd fight it off. It was good, being among people who obviously shared a common bond. But I wasn't ready to cry like a baby and that's what it felt like I was about to do."

Somehow Bo managed to keep his cool. Listening to his fellow inmates he intellectualized that alcoholics and drug addicts go through an especially difficult time during the holidays Listening to the others gave him some insight into what he had been feeling and experiencing over the past few weeks. "Holidays scared me," he reports. "The only difference between this one and those in the past twelve years was that this time I wasn't gonna stay numb and avoid everyone."

The usual custom at an AA meeting is to conclude by joining hands and saying the Lord's Prayer. But it was Christmas and the leader suggested that they join hands, turn out the lights, and sing "Silent Night."

" Hesitant voices began to join one another, a joyous noise began to be born. Soon every man in that moonlit room was lifting his voice. A ragged lot of society's outcasts—thieves, murderers, rapists—were holding hands in the dark and singing."

And that's when it happened for Bo. That's when God happened for Bo and it changed his life. This is how he remembers it: "Those emotions I'd been feeling all day came back. This time, though, in the dark and surrounded by voices of God's children, it was okay. I let my guard down. As the tears flowed down my face, a warmth spread all over my entire body. Bathed in this glorious, healing presence, I suddenly knew: God was real. Not only was he real, but he was in the room with us."

As the lights came back on, Bo discovered that he wasn't the only prisoner wiping his eyes. This was a new beginning for Bo. He had begun a new journey. It took him a while to find out who Jesus was and he's still learning who Jesus is. It was a while before he was willing to tell anyone that he is a Christian, but the journey had begun.

As it turned out, there was another correspondent who was also receiving mail from Bo. Her name was Deborah. She was the secretary at Christ Episcopal Church, Richmond, Kentucky. Sorting out the mail one morning, she came across a mailing from Forward Movement Publications. It was promoting *Release,* a special edition of Bo's first set of meditations. On the flyer was Bo's picture, and according to Deborah it was love at first sight. She wrote a letter to Bo via the publisher. The letter was delivered by the prison chaplain and the correspondence began. A month later she was on a bus to Oklahoma to meet Bo. A year later Deborah, her parents, and her brother-in-law who was a clergyman waited in the County Court House for Bo to be brought in prison uniform, handcuffs, and leg irons to sign the marriage application. Then it was back to the prison in Holdenville where, along with twelve other couples, Deborah and Bo exchanged their marriage vows. The couple never had a honeymoon, nor are they ever allowed any privacy. When Deborah makes her weekly visit, they meet in a room with other couples under the ever-present eyes of the prison guards.

Bo is now considered a model prisoner. In addition to his work in the clinic, he is often given leave (under guard) to speak in high schools and universities. The reports are that he is very effective. He is an excellent example of the rehabilitated convict. There is a small group of us who are working on his behalf for parole, and Deborah Cox, who lives and works in Norman, Oklahoma, is coordinating the efforts with the parole board. We believe that Bo has much to contribute to society, but we understand, and Bo understands, that he may well spend the rest of his life behind bars. He says that he can endure that as long as the Lord is with him.

During one of Bo's speaking engagements before a class of sociology students, he, and a fellow inmate, Tom, were confronted by a very angry woman who felt that prisoners had it too easy and that they should be "punished, not helped." Bo struggled for an answer. For eight years he had been locked up in an oversized dog pen, "stuck out in the woods where society didn't have to look at me. Couldn't she see I *was* being punished?" His anger was beginning to rise when Tom whispered in his ear, "Mercy triumphs over judgment."

Scripture

You do well if you really fulfill the royal law according to the scripture, "You shall love your neighbor as yourself." But if you show partiality, you commit sin and are convicted by the law as transgressors. For whoever keeps the whole law but fails in one point has become accountable for all of it. For the one who said, "You shall not commit adultery," also said, "You shall not murder." Now if you do not commit adultery, but if you murder, you have become a transgressor of the

*law. So speak and so act as those who are to be judged by the law of
liberty. For judgment will be without mercy to anyone who has shown
no mercy; mercy triumphs over judgment.*

James 2:8-13
NRSV

Reflection

The passage from the Letter of James, selected by Bo Cox, has both
good news and bad. On the one hand it condemns sin in no uncertain
terms and on the other it commends mercy.

Most of the people who I know, including myself, think that the Bible
is talking about someone else when it mentions sin. For Bo, there was
no question that this passage's reference to murder referred to him. He
stood convicted, both in a court of law and under the Torah of God. No
question about it! No wiggle room there! But James also speaks of
mercy: God's mercy and the mercy we are to show one another.

The cross of Christ was not planted on a marble altar between two
silver candles. It was planted on a hill outside the city wall between two
convicted criminals. To the one who turned to Jesus, he said, "You will
be with me. Now! Today!"

No wonder Bo cried when they sang Silent Night. Not only did the
memories of Christmases past come rushing in; not only could he
remember lighting the candles in a darkened church on Christmas Eve;
but he realized that the "loves pure light" was for him. No wonder he
cried. Tears are a wonderful thing. As every Sunday school student
knows, even "Jesus wept." The Psalmist (56:8) declares that God keeps
our "tears in a bottle." I have a very dear friend, Jean MacPherson, who
says that, "tears are an inner baptism," a spiritual cleansing. Bo's tears
mourned his lost innocence. They cried out in grief for the life he had

taken. They also cried for joy, realizing that even he, a convicted murderer, was loved by God.

A good question for personal reflection might be, "How long has it been since I've had a good cry?"

Hymn

Silent night, holy night,
All is calm, all is bright.
Round yon virgin mother and child.
Holy infant so tender and mild,
Sleep in heavenly peace.
Sleep in heavenly peace.

Silent night, holy night,
Shepherds quake at the sight,
Glories stream from heaven afar,
Heavenly hosts sing alleluia;
Christ, the savior, is born!
Christ, the savior, is born!

Silent night, holy night,
Son of God, love's pure light.
Radiant beams from his holy face,
With the dawn of redeeming grace,
Jesus, Lord at thy birth.
Jesus, Lord, at thy birth.

Franz Xaver Gruber 1818
1982 Episcopal Hymnal, #111

Chapter Three

Under The Bridge

Terry Maria Smythe

The law is impartial. There is equal justice under the law. It is illegal for both rich and poor to sleep under bridges. In Florida it is also illegal for a person to sleep in an automobile, unless the car is parked in an official rest area. That law applies equally to the well-to-do and the homeless.

At the intersection of Biscayne Boulevard and I-195 in Miami, Florida, a chain link fence encloses a large area beneath the overpass that takes traffic to and from Miami Beach. Back in the winter of 1991 a late model car pulled off the road and a forty-something woman wearing designer shoes stepped on to the sandy soil. She surveyed the area, noting the 24 hour Denny's restaurant nearby, the Taco Bell on the corner, and the Police Museum across the street. Maybe this would be a safe place. For Terry Smythe this was a whole new world, totally foreign to suburban Westchester County world she knew best. Through the mist of her own depression Terry was beginning to focus on the fact that she was now homeless. The heels of her Italian Ferragamo shoes began to disappear into the sandy soil as the reality of her new condition sank into her psyche.

Terry was baptized Theresa Maria Smythe. She was the daughter of an English businessman and a South American lady whose roots went back to the conquistadors of Central America. As a child she had learned English and Spanish simultaneously. She addressed her poppa in English and her madre in Castillian Spanish. She grew up mostly in South America and at age 11 was sent off to a proper boarding school in

England. She continued her education in Italy and South America, in Massachusetts, and finally at Columbia University, New York City where she earned a masters degree and worked on a Ph.D. in international relations. By this time she spoke English, Spanish, French, and Italian. In Boston, through family friends, she met and became engaged to Spencer, scion of an old New England family. Together she and Spence built a business and accumulated all the trappings of a successful upper class American family. They purchased a five acre wooded tract in Westchester County where they designed and built a spacious home. They entertained lavishly, joined the country club, and raised two children. The only thing missing from the model family portrait was church.

Terry had been baptized in the Roman Catholic Church in South America, where she also made her first communion and was confirmed before leaving for England. At that point her father's Church of England tradition took over and she learned how to navigate through the 1662 Book of Common Prayer in the school chapel. Terry wasn't religious, nor was she anti-religious; she simply was not religious. Church and chapel were just something one went to or through like school assembly, the Queen's birthday in England, or, in the United States, a traditional Fourth of July parade. She and Spence had been married in a Roman Catholic Church, but she didn't attend mass. Spence's family had an Episcopal background, but he never went to church.

When Terry gave birth to her second child she almost died. She remembers sensing that she was dying. She remembers being drawn toward a soft light and thinking, "I must be dying and it isn't all that bad. There must be a God after all." She heard the heart monitor go flat and the code blue alarm go off. The delivery room nurse bent over her and smacked her across the face and yelled, "Fight, damn it, fight!" Somewhat reluctantly she came back to the pain of her body and the land of the living. But the experience had no lasting effect on her spiritual life. Her intellect took over and rationalized the whole experience, or at least neutralized its impact. When they built their home and their children were small, they dropped them off at Sunday school at a nearby Episcopal parish. But even that vague connection dissolved as the Holmes' social schedule became more and more demanding. Neither Terry, nor her family, felt any great spiritual need.

And then the marriage and business partnership, which began as a dream, became a nightmare. The process of divorce was under way. The court had ordered Spence to maintain the house, pay the bills, and provide Terry with a reasonable allowance, but things had gotten nasty. There were fights. She was punched in the stomach, kicked, and bounced off the wall. "There is nothing more horrendous than looking into the eyes of someone you have lain next to in bed and seeing hatred," she said. "It's horrible."

One of Terry's friends had gone through a divorce and almost lost her life when her husband hired a hit man who fortunately was in charge of an FBI sting operation. Spence, after a few drinks, would tell Terry that he wouldn't make that kind of mistake. He'd find a hit man with a high batting average. "Sometime when I'm out on the West Coast," he declared, "he hit man will break into the house, steal some silver, and bash your f——ing head in with the fireplace poker. You'll be dead and nobody will be able to pin it on me."

When it became evident that domestic relations cases were backing up and that court orders weren't being enforced, business assets began to disappear and Spence stopped paying the electric bills, discontinued the landscaping service, and had the locks taken off the doors. Terry went to bed in terror every night. Somehow the idea of being murdered in her sleep was the most frightening thought of all. Unable to lock the doors, each night she would build a pyramid of coke cans inside her door. Someone entering her house would have to knock over the cans and she would at least be awake to confront her assassin.

In such a state of mind Terry took off for Florida. Upon arrival, she discovered that the bank had foreclosed on her house and that her credit cards had been canceled. She was stranded with only a few dollars in her purse and a car with a half-tank of gas and her friends in Miami were out of town. She considered the Salvation Army, but somehow images of uniformed lassies tending their Christmas kettles and ringing their bells on Fifth Avenue outside of Bergdorf Goodman's turned her off. Besides, she incorrectly imagined that she would have to "get saved" before they would feed her or give her a bed for the night. She considered sleeping in her car. She had heard of homeless women using the rest rooms along the Merritt Parkway in Connecticut and sleeping in the parking areas, but in Miami there are no designated rest areas. along I-95. What about shopping malls? That's illegal in Florida and is extremely dangerous. You can get trapped in a car; robbed in a car; raped in a car.

So there she stood surveying the scene when a huge black man approached and asked for a cigarette. Terry had only a few Marlboros left. She handed the man one and they shared a light. He wondered what she was doing there. Was she a reporter? Was she someone from the sheriff's office? A lady detective wouldn't wear shoes like the ones she had on, would she? Maybe she was a do-gooder or a lady bountiful from Coral Gables, Aventura, or Fisher Island? Maybe she could help him out with a little bit of money?

But Terry was none of the above. She was looking for a place to spend the night. No, she wasn't looking for someone to spend the night with. "I'm afraid I'm homeless and I need a safe place to spend the night," Terry stated as matter-of-factly as she could.

"You want to stay away from the folks on that corner," he said pointing in a north westerly direction. "That's where the druggies hang out." Then he pointed to a grungy old overstuffed armchair. " Maybe that will do."

Terry got within three feet of the chair and pulled back. The lingering odor of former tenants was pungent and offensive. "I'd rather put some paper on the ground and sleep there."

The black man nodded his agreement. "That's no place for a lady," he said. He then introduced her to two street people, Bo and Christine. Bo was an average-sized Afro-American with a lot of street smarts. He had a lot of personal charm and a winning smile. He was something of a con man. Christine was a pathetically thin Anglo with dirty blonde hair and a haunted look about her. They were an odd couple but they became Terry's protectors, her guardian angels, and they introduced her to a world she had never even imagined existed. Her course in "street skills" was about to begin. As the shadows lengthened, a little community gathered and preparations were made for supper. There were about thirty people in all under the bridge. Half were in the druggie group and the other dozen or so gathered around Terry. Whatever had been begged, borrowed, liberated, scrounged, or stolen was placed on the surface of a flattened cardboard box which became the dining room table. Terry was introduced around. "She's under my personal protection," announced Bo. "Anybody touches her is going to have to answer to me. Put that word out. Nobody hurts or takes anything from this lady."

Life under the bridge reduced existence to its basics. There was the matter of going to the toilet. Denny's and Taco Bell discouraged street people from using their facilities. Terry managed to get by most of the time. She still had some cash with which she could order a cup of coffee, occupy a booth, and slip into the ladies room, remembering to load up on toilet paper to share with Bo, Christine, and other members of the community. Keeping one's clothing clean and fresh was an equally challenging. There was also the problem of bathing. Terry could manage that in the rest room at Denny's, while the others had to slip into the brackish waters of Biscayne Bay late at night. Terry managed to rinse out her undergarments in the restroom but the others weren't as lucky with their clothing. She remembers a former Eastern Airlines' pilot who joined their little community. When the Miami based air line went belly up, many of the pilots and crew members were hired by other carriers who rushed into the Southeastern hub to fill the gates left vacant by Eastern and Pan Am. George was not so lucky. He was in that age limbo where he was too young for his pension and too old to be hired. The collapse of Eastern had also triggered the end of his marriage. His few assets had quickly dissolved in a sea of litigation and court orders. George tried his best to keep one suit of clothing presentable so that he could go out and look for a job. He searched the help wanted ads in newspapers that he salvaged from trash barrels. He tried the supermarkets and drug stores, minimum wage jobs, whatever. The answer always seemed to be, "You're over qualified."

Then there was Henry, an Afro-American, who did not speak Spanish. He would leave before first light, go to Trinity Cathedral or some other downtown church for breakfast, and stand on the "casual labor corner" where local contractors picked up hungry workers willing to grunt and sweat for a day's pay. Often the contractors or foremen who came to the corner spoke only Spanish and so Henry would not be hired. But when he was able to get a day's work, he would put a lot of his meager pay into the grocery pool. Then he would go down to the bay to wash his sweaty clothing. In Miami it's against the law to bathe or wash one's clothing in public. Henry was eventually arrested and dumped over the county line.

Food gathering was always a challenge. Dumpsters near fast food outlets usually provided a supply of half-eaten meals. The ones behind Kentucky Fried Chicken often had unconsumed mashed potatoes, gravy, coleslaw, and crunchy fried chicken skins, wings, and bones. Sometimes, late at night, the dumpster behind Denny's would contain whole plastic bags of unserved salad bar items.

There was no cooking under the bridge, because a fire would bring the police. Although it was against the law, local authorities at that time refused to give food stamps to the homeless because they had no place to cook. Those who had money could buy day old bread, peanut butter and jelly. Liquids were a big problem. There was no supply of water nearby; no outside faucets that could be turned on at night, and the local merchants chased the homeless off during the day. Sometimes the dumpsters or trash cans had half full containers of Coke or coffee. Sometimes not, but what they had they shared in common. Everyone looked forward to supper on Saturday evening when a caravan of utility vehicles from a large Bahamian church delivered a full meal served on clean paper plates, with plastic forks, paper napkins—and desert.

Little by little Terry settled into the routine of life under the bridge. Like the characters in a Dostoevsky novel, everyone had at least two names. There was the street name and then there was a person's real name. The real name was kept private and only shared with people you could trust. It was as if people were saying, "This really isn't happening to me." Bo's real name was Willie. Terry was known as "The Reader." She discovered a public library within walking distance. They discouraged homeless people as much as they could, but at first anyway Terry didn't look homeless, so she could enjoy the air conditioning, water fountains, and bathrooms, as well as the reading material. This worked until she asked for a library card. The librarian refused her request on the grounds that she didn't have a local address. Fortunately Terry had been researching homelessness and was able to quote chapter and verse of Florida law that protected the rights of homeless people. When she indicated her willingness to go to the TV stations with her problem, she got her library card.

By this time, she had made her peace with the overstuffed chair, covered it daily with fresh newspaper and/or cardboard, and would read early in the morning and in the evening. At her side was a slightly deformed black and white "Tuxedo" cat who had adopted her and allowed her to share the couch. Sometimes Terry would read the news of the day to the assembled community while Tuxedo presided over the gathering with a superior air.

It was from this assembled community of obviously flawed and imperfect people that Terry discovered something she had never known before. Somehow God became real. Her life up to that point had been totally agnostic. OK, there might be a God, but on the other hand she could just as easily say, "How do you know there is a God or what proof do you have of God's existence-anyway, what difference does it make! But under the bridge Terry came to the conclusion that there is a God and that he is good. Now, some eight years later, she shakes her head and wonders how, under those terrible circumstances she could have come to the conclusion that God is good. "Maybe," she says, "it was the reflection of goodness that I saw in those people who were so obviously imperfect, which enabled me to see the goodness of God."

Terry stayed under the bridge in Miami for two months before moving on. In the Washington, DC area she was not as fortunate as she had been under the bridge in Miami. She was raped in a parking lot and then confined in the mental health ward of a local public hospital. Eventually she was rescued by old friends and discovered by the media. When the nightmare of homelessness was over, Terry found her way into a church. She was drawn to the Gospels, to the person of Jesus, to the Book of Psalms, to prayer, and to the Lord's Table. She also became an articulate advocate for battered women and especially for women thrown into poverty as a result of divorce. She appeared on almost all of the local New York stations as well as network programs such as: Montel Williams, Maurie Povitch, Geraldo Rivera, and 48 Minutes. A German TV production company featured her in a documentary on homelessness in America, portions of which were shown at the Beijing Woman's Conference in 1994. She takes pride in the fact that through her story, laws were changed "to level the playing field" in domestic relations cases. She is now living on Key Biscayne, serving on the altar guild at St. Christopher's by-the-Sea, and assisting as a grant writer for a homeless shelter. She says," I can pray for the men who raped me, and hope that they are off drugs. I pray that they never rape anyone else. I pray for my husband and I wish him great happiness."

And Terry has a cat. It's an old cat and it a black and white cat. It wandered into the homeless shelter one day when she was working on a grant application. It was very thin and in bad shape. She brought it home. Is it Tuxedo? "Who knows," says Terry, " but that wouldn't be the only miracle that happened under the bridge."

Scripture

Lord, hear my prayer,
and in your faithfulness heed my supplications;
answer me in your righteousness.

Enter not into judgment with your servant,
for in your sight shall no one living be justified.

For my enemy has sought my life;
he has crushed me to the ground;
he has made me live in dark places like those who
are long dead.

My spirit faints within me;
my heart within me is desolate.

I remember the time past;
I muse upon all your deeds;
I consider the works of your hands.

I spread out my hands to you;
my soul gasps to you like a thirsty land.

O Lord make haste to answer me; my spirit fails me;
do not hide your face from me

or I shall be like those who go down to the Pit.

Let me hear of your loving kindness in the morning,
for I put my trust in you;
Show me the road that I must walk,
for I lift up my soul to you.

Deliver me from my enemies, O Lord,
for I flee to you in refuge.

Teach me to do what pleases you, for you are my God;
let your good spirit lead me on level ground.

Revive me, O lord, for your Name's sake;
for your righteousness' sake, bring me out of trouble.

'Psalm 143: 1-11
1979 Book of Common Prayer

Reflection

When I read Terry's selection from the Book of Psalms, I was struck by how closely it paralleled her own experience. The Psalmist writing almost three millenniums ago had felt the same things, uttered the same cry. He had been there and done that. The Bible is filled with all kinds of surprises like that.

While Terry would not wish her homeless experience even on her ex-husband, she came out of that phase of her life with a deep appreciation for the redemptive quality of human suffering. She recalls a conversation she had with the Jewish author, Elie Wiesel, who has written so eloquently about the experience of the Holocaust. One of Wiesel's recurring themes is the "power of one." When you talk about what is happening to millions of people, people won't understand. When you talk about what happened to you, they will listen. This encouraged Terry to speak out, to go public with her story in the hope that others would be helped by it. The second thing she learned from Wiesel was the redemptive quality of suffering. Wiesel didn't believe that suffering is redemptive. He believed that suffering all too often erodes and corrodes the soul. "There's nothing good about it," he contended. Terry agreed at first. Homelessness had taken it toll, but it did not destroy her. In many ways she saw herself as a better person. It brought her to faith.

Suffering can lead to bitterness, but it can also lead to one becoming a more caring, loving and sensitive person. "Look at Elie Weisel," she says, "Look at what a great soul he has!" Reading the story of Joseph in Genesis helped Terry sort this out. Scripture declares that "The Lord was with Joseph." A good question for reflection on our own suffering is "Where is the Lord in all of this?"

Hymn

I want to walk as a child of the light.
I want to follow Jesus.
God set the stars to give light to the world.
The star of my life is Jesus.

Refrain

In him there is no darkness at all.
The night and the day are both alike.
The lamb is the light of the city of God.
Shine in my heart, Lord Jesus.

Refrain

I want to see the brightness of God.
I want to look at Jesus.
Clear sun of righteousness, shine on my path,
and show me the way to the Father.

Refrain

I'm looking for the coming of Christ.
I want to be with Jesus.
When we have run with patience—with patience the race,
We shall know the joy-of Jesus.

Refrain

Kathleen Thomerson (b. 1934)
1982 Episcopal Hymnal, #490

Chapter Four

Leadership Under Pressure

Frank T. Griswold

Two days after my official retirement party and final service as rector of St. Christopher's by-the-Sea, Key Biscayne, Florida, I was on a plane from Miami International to New York. The flight marked a point of transition from parish priest and headmaster to writer, conference leader, and sometime religious journalist. It was a smooth transition as well as a smooth flight. I had an appointment that afternoon to interview Frank Tracy Griswold, who had just marked the first anniversary of his election in 1997 to the office of Presiding Bishop.

The election of a Presiding Bishop for the Episcopal Church is not quite as dramatic as the election of a Pope, but it comes close. At least it comes close if you happen to be a member of the Episcopal Church; and it's especially exciting if you're part of the press corps covering the event.

In Philadelphia in 1997, the Episcopal Church elected a new presiding bishop at the General Convention. My wife, Lynne was a deputy from Southeast Florida and I was reporting for *The Living Church*, an American weekly religious magazine, and the *Church of England Newspaper*, a weekly tabloid serving the UK.

The process involves election by the House of Bishops and confirmation by the elected clergy and lay deputies in the House of Deputies. After the nominating committee has made it's report and presented a slate of nominees and additional nominations have been made from the floor, the bishops went behind closed doors to pray for the guidance of the Holy Spirit and ballot until someone had a majority. The bishops' selection is then brought back to the "lower house" for ratification.

At the Philadelphia meeting, it seemed appropriate that the successors to the apostles gather in the nearby historic Christ Church. It was there in 1789 that the Episcopal Church in the United States, having declared its own independence from the Church of England, met in General Convention to draft and adopt its constitution and canons and to authorize an American *Book of Common Prayer*. And it was in Philadelphia that the Continental Congress also gathered for prayer in 1789—and to begin hammering out the plans for a new government.

The term "paparazzi" was not in circulation at the time of Bishop Griswold's election, but we had a close facsimile. Rick Wood, moonlighting from the *Milwaukee Journal Sentinel*, climbed up a tree outside of Christ Church and with a telefoto lens through a clear glass window photographed the bishops placing their ballots in a box. He also caught Bishop Griswold standing at the church door shaking hands with a number of bishops as the bishops adjourned. That was enough for *The Living Church*. When the results of the election were officially brought to the House of Deputies three hours later, Rick's plane was circling the Milwaukee Airport. By the time he had developed his pictures and brought them to the office of *The Living Church*, the story had been written and E-mailed to Milwaukee. In fact David Kalvelage, the editor, had already received the page proofs by FAX in Philadelphia and sent them back to Milwaukee. By 10:00 am the next day, 1,000 copies of the magazine were being distributed to the Convention, with the picture of the Presiding Bishop Elect on the front cover in living color. His name: Frank T. Griswold. He had been, for the past 10 years, Bishop of Chicago. When Frank Griswold preached his first sermon at the Convention as Presiding Bishop Elect, I tried my hand at the paparazzi bit and was a complete failure. Finding myself sitting cross legged on the floor in front of the V.I.P section, I spotted Phoebe Griswold, the bishop's wife, hanging on her husband's every word. "What a shot," I thought, and aimed my camera, framing Phoebe, in sharp focus in the foreground gazing adoringly at her husband in the pulpit. When everyone stood up to sing a hymn, I slipped quietly out the door and dashed down the street to an instant photo-processing establishment. An hour later the film came back. It was completely blank. "That's been happening a lot today," said the clerk. "There must be something wrong with the machine. The boss said to give you another roll of film. I hope it wasn't anything important!" So much for the award winning photo of the year! I decided that in the future I had better stick to writing.

On July 7, 1998, Bishop Griswold had been in office for barely six months. He jokingly referred to "six months and ten pounds later." The stated purpose for our meeting was to produce an article for the *Church of England Newspaper* on the man who in two weeks would lead the Episcopal Church USA delegation of 130 bishops to the Lambeth Conference at Canterbury. The article appeared in the July 17 issue of CEN, on the eve of the opening service. The headline read, "Why we Americans appear to be arrogant." He was advising his fellow countrymen to "assume the stance of listener—and be ready to receive ....We shouldn't assume that what we think and feel is normative. We should be ready to enter into conversation."

Conversation had turned out to be a key word in his public ministry as well as his personal life. It has the same root as the word *conversion*. "Conversation," said Griswold, "means listening in such a way that I am open to the possibility of being changed or expanded by what I hear you say."

But, I was not only in New York to write an article for a church newspaper, I was beginning to gather material for this book and so I asked the Presiding Bishop the basic question asked in this book, "How did you become a Christian?"

Frank Griswold hadn't always been a bishop or even a priest, but he couldn't ever

remember a time when he didn't identify himself as a Christian.

He was born into an upper middle class family in suburban Philadelphia and shortly after his birth he was baptized on January 1, 1938. What he describes as being an "active and self aware Christian," did not occur until he got away from home and went off to boarding school in Concord, New Hampshire. At St. Paul's he found himself in the choir and was "exposed to the full life of the church." He was fascinated by the power of the liturgy, the daily round of Morning Prayer and Evensong, along with the sacrament of Holy Communion. He learned the strange names for the chants: *Kyrie, Sanctus, Nunc dimittis, Magnificat,* etc. He also learned their meaning. This "drew him toward Christ." When the time came for his class to be presented to the bishop to claim the vows taken in their name at their baptism, he held back for a year. And while he did not give "much thought to being confirmed," this was a significant period in his spiritual development. He remembers receiving a book, *God's Presence.* It was a devotional book in the High Church or Anglo-Catholic tradition and contained the order for Morning and Evening Prayer as well as a form for making a confession. There were also private prayers to be said in conjunction with the Eucharist and explanations for the ritual of the service. It struck him as "completely right and completely logical." Frank Griswold made it a part of his spiritual life, which he describes as "active and intense." He learned to pray both formally and informally. One of the school chaplains, noting that he "was more devout than most of the other boys" suggested that he seek spiritual direction. At age 15 he was put in touch with the Cowley Fathers at the Society of St. John the Evangelist in Cambridge, Massachusetts, who saw him through his prep school years and college days at Harvard. He remembers a very kind and understanding priest, Fr. Alfred Patterson, who took his "adolescent religious fervor" and gently guided him in "the nicest possible way." Fr. Patterson became a "surrogate father."

While he was still at St. Paul's, Griswold made the decision to seek ordination. It came about in a strange way. One evening his roommate came back from a faculty tea, laughing his head off. "You'll never guess," he reported, "what one of the teachers said at tea this afternoon. He said that 'Griswold should go into the church.'" They both doubled over with laughter. The Presiding Bishop likened that moment to his "annunciation." It certainly wasn't like Gabriel's announcement to Mary, and he thought it was "so bizarre and shocking" that he decided to "play along with it." This initial fascination with a strange idea eventually "matured into a sense of vocation." In his college years at Harvard the vocation to priesthood was "tested" on every level. Fortunately he was within walking distance of the Cowley Fathers and more specifically he had the friendship, prayers, and counsel of Fr. Patterson.

His theological education began at the General Theological Seminary in New York and was completed at Oriel College at Oxford University in England. Again it was with the assistance of a wise and caring spiritual director that he was able to maneuver the eccentricities of the Church of England.

A major part of Frank Griswold's spiritual formation and center rests in the discipline of St. Benedict and his followers, which encourages a balanced life of worship, study, and work. For the non-cloistered associate, it involves reading the daily offices of Morning and Evening Prayer as well as placing oneself under spiritual direction.

For more than thirty years Griswold has followed this discipline and made an annual retreat to Mount Savior, a Benedictine monastery in Elmira, New York. It was at such a retreat in the late 1970's that he felt that he was taken apart and then put back together again.

"There was me, the Bible, and a spiritual director with whom I met for an hour each day over an eight day period." Part of the structure of the retreat was to enter into scripture under the guidance of the Holy Spirit, and to let the Holy Spirit "accost you" as you find yourself becoming one of the apostles in the story, letting Jesus address you directly. Using this discipline the scriptures came to life. The director then told Griswold to, "Ask Jesus to show you what gifts he has given you." That sounded like an easy assignment, but when the answer came back from Jesus, "You have nothing!" he was devastated. "I was in shock—absolute shock." But, he trusted that this was from the Lord and not from some "malevolent spirit." and stayed with the process and then received the reassuring word from the Lord, "You have my love and my grace. That's all!" He had the incredible sense of being utterly naked and incredibly poor and overwhelmed by the experience. It was a fundamental experience of grace. He found himself, no longer determined by his own perspective, "but rather finding myself embraced by mercy....an ongoing awareness of the compassion of God which was so much more welcoming than we could ever be to ourselves." From that defining moment he believes that, "We can only welcome ourselves and others in a deep, deep way as we enter into God's compassion and see each other from that perspective and see ourselves from that perspective." That conviction has been with him for a long time now and keeps being reconfirmed.

Scripture

Therefore, to keep me from being too elated, a thorn was given me in the flesh, a messenger of Satan to torment me, to keep me from being too elated. Three times I appealed to the Lord about this, that it would leave me, but he said to me, "My grace is sufficient for you, for power is made perfect in weakness." So, I will boast all the more gladly of my weaknesses, so that the power of Christ may dwell in me. Therefore I am content with weaknesses, insults, hardships, persecutions, and calamities for the sake of Christ; for whenever I am weak, then I am strong.

2 Corinthians 12:7-10
NRSV

Reflection

While much that went on at Lambeth was reported in the press and posted on the internet, the most significant part of Lambeth for most of the bishops was the daily Bible story. Under the broad heading of "Leadership Under Pressure," the Archbishop of Canterbury had chosen the Second letter of St. Paul to the Corinthians for the community's reflection and "conversation". Each day's session was preceded by a video clip with a personal comment or story by one of the bishops. On the morning that the above passage was under consideration, a bishop from the Sudan, Nathaniel Garang Angieth of the Diocese of Bor, spoke of the civil war which has raged in his homeland. He said that shortly after he was consecrated a bishop that he was isolated and completely cut off from the rest of the church in Sudan. Not only was there no financial support for his missionary work, but there was no personal or spiritual contact with the larger church . "The Bishop in Tuba thought I was dead," he said. During the six years of isolation that followed, he went about the job he had been given to do. He trained and ordained 75 pastors and established 150 churches. "God helped and directed me in many ways. God was all I had." He certainly knew the meaning of "My grace is sufficient for you."

We are told as Christians that there is such a thing as God's grace. We don't deserve it. We can't earn it or buy it. It's a free gift. It's there for us in Holy Scripture, in prayer, in worship, in the sacraments, in community with other Christians, in listening and in conversation, in responding to the needs of others, and in a thousand, make that a million, opportunities for service.

We're told that God's grace is really all we need, not only for survival, but for a full and meaningful life.

In my own spiritual journey I have discovered three words that unlock the power of God's grace. They are forgiveness, thanksgiving, and faith. Forgiveness is God's grace to cut us loose from the sins or hurts of the past and a way of living in an imperfect world. Thanksgiving liberates us from the successes of the past and enables us to identify and appreciate God's grace in the present. Faith is the trust that God's grace will be there for us in the future; that it will be sufficient for us no matter what.

In our baptismal vows, right after we say that we accept Jesus Christ as our savior, we are asked if we will put our "whole trust in his grace and love." When we are able to say that, then we are ready to promise to follow him as Lord.

Hymn

Come, my Way, my Truth, my Life:
such a way as gives us breath;
such a truth as ends all strife;
such a life as killeth death.

Come, my Light, my Feast, my Strength:
such a light as shows a feast;
such a feast as mends in length;
such a strength as makes his guest.

Come, my Joy, my Love, my Heart:
such a joy as none can move;
such a love as none can part;
such a heart as joys in love.

George Herbert (1593-1633)
1982 Episcopal Hymnal,#487

Chapter Five

Amen Court

Michael Saward

Two weeks after my visit with Bishop Griswold, I looked out of my plane window and watched the first light of a new day break over Ireland. An hour later they were checking my luggage through customs at London's Gatwick Airport. Two hours after that I was being greeted by Michael and Jackie Saward at Number Six Amen Court. Amen Court is the "close" or courtyard that houses the clergy residences for St. Paul's Cathedral. Michael is one of the senior canons in residence.

Michael Saward is one of those rare commodities called "a friend for life." It all began in the summer of 1968. I was the newly appointed radio and television officer for the Episcopal Church in the United States and Michael had just been assigned to the same post with the Church of England. We were thrown together on the communication staff for a gathering of Anglican bishops from around the world. The bishops were convened by the Archbishop of Canterbury. It has happened every ten years and it is called the Lambeth Conference. The name of the Conference refers to a time when there were fewer bishops and they could all be housed at Lambeth Palace, the Archbishop's London residence, upstream from the Houses of Parliament.

For the first week we competed fiercely with each other until we realized that there was only one job to be done and that it would be half the work and twice the fun if we worked at it together. One weekend Michael and I rented a car and we drove—I should say he drove because

I was terrified by the idea of driving on the wrong side of the road—out to Ross-on-Wye, a sheep herding town, north of Bristol and close to the Welsh border. It was there that my "Nana," my grandmother, had been born. Fortunately, the clerk of the parish church was available and showed me the entry of my grandmother's baptism, *Alice Mercer Hill* in 1876. I ordered photocopies of the church register and sketches of St. Mary's Church, which I duly sent to family members near and far.

On the way back, we spent the night at Michael's theological college in Bristol. Tyndale Hall, later renamed Trinity, prided itself on being in the Evangelical tradition of the Church of England. George Carey, later to become the 103rd Archbishop of Canterbury, was principal of the college from 1982 to 1987. I arose early on Sunday morning to attend Holy Communion at nearby All Saints Church, which was as "catholic" as Trinity College was "evangelical." The building was of a very contemporary "church in the round design," attached to an ancient gothic bell tower, which was all of the original structure to be left standing after the German bombs had done their nasty work in World War II. The new sanctuary had been constructed with the rubble from the original building, and it was to the credit of the architects that I couldn't detect where the old left off and the new began. Michael insisted on taking me to a later service at the leading Evangelical church in Bath, which could barely contain the crowd. The same thing happened that evening back in London, when Michael insisted that we hear the Rev. John Stott at All Souls', Langham Place. We found two seats on the back row in the balcony. It was a hot August night. Michael and I were in our mid thirties, but it felt like we were among the more senior members of the congregation.

Michael was definitely an Evangelical and proud of it. As such he was elected for twenty years to the General Church Synod (national ruling body) and was a major player in passing the legislation to allow for the ordination of women to the priesthood. He had been vicar of two large London parishes. He was a prolific hymn writer and in 1991 received a crown appointment to be a senior canon at St. Paul's Cathedral, London. In 1999 his twelfth book and autobiography, *A faint streak of humility*, was published and reviewed in almost all of the major secular newspapers. Tragically, he is most often identified in the British press as the cleric whose house was burgled and daughter raped. I told that story in *The Forgiveness Book* so I won't repeat it here.

Young Michael Saward, age 12, slept on a narrow bunk in the family air raid shelter in the garden behind his home at Pettswood, some twelve miles southeast of London. It was the summer of 1944 and although the possibility of a Nazi defeat increased every day, the war wasn't over yet. Seeking shelter in the back yard had become a nightly ritual for the young lad, his mum and baby sister. The Allies might be advancing in Europe, but barely a week after the Normandy landing, the German V-1 flying bombs had begun to cross the Channel heading for London. Michael had learned to listen: first for the snarl of their engines, then a cough followed by an eerie silence, and then the dreadful explosion. Everyone knew that as long as you could hear the engine droning, you were OK. It's when they stopped that it was time to be worried. Michael and his friends called them "doodle bugs" others called them "buzz bombs." Michael lay awake at midnight and the doodle bugs were coming over, some to the left and some to the right. He held his breath as he heard one approaching dead center. Would it pass over head and continue on its route to the center city? They heard the roar as the bomb came closer and closer, and then there was silence. Michael waited for what seemed like an eternity for the explosion. But then there was a sputtering and the flash of a yellowish light as the engine restarted for about ten seconds. There was a second silence and then the explosion. A neighbor up the road had watched the whole thing from his front porch and thought, since the nose of the rocket was heading down to their house, "that's the end of the Sawards!" Then, he reported that the engine fired again, passed over the house, and landed in a farmyard a half mile away. It killed two cows and left a large crater, which in due time became a fish pond.

Reflecting on the event some fifty years later, Michael Saward could not resist the temptation to draw a parallel to John Wesley's being rescued from his father's burning rectory when he was a young lad. Those were Michael's thoughts after more than forty years in the priesthood and eight years as a canon at St. Paul's Cathedral in London, but at age twelve the narrow escape was seen as a piece of luck prompting his being evacuated to a safer venue, far away from London, at the home of Auntie Alice and her husband Jack in the north of England.

Michael's family could not be considered a religious one although if pressed, they would, like most English people at that time regard themselves as "Christian" and, of course, Church of England. They had taken Michael as a baby to the parish church to be baptized, but that was it. Michael remembers an occasional church visit for a christening, wedding, or funeral, and once a year he recalls his mother attended a three-hour Good Friday service. Except for the experience of school chapel, which he described as being "without a shred of any spiritual vitality," Michael knew nothing of a traditional Christian upbringing, Sunday school, or church life. But at age eleven, much to his own surprise and that of everyone else who knew him, Michael, who liked to sing, joined the choir at the local parish church, St. Francis, Pettswood. Although it was a rather austere experience, and a far cry form the evangelical tradition that later shaped his spiritual life, he stayed with it for three years and received a penny a Sunday for his musical efforts. Trying to visualize the scene, it has the comical air of one of those wartime Britcoms, with a choir of elderly men and women, and a handful of prepubescent lads being led by a rather tousled and somewhat dotty old vicar. During the 36 months of attendance, he can only remember one notable sermon, delivered not by the vicar, but by a visiting missionary.

Michael dates his spiritual awakening and coming to faith to an invitation, when he was thirteen, to attend a camp run by the Crusaders, a boy's Bible class organization. It was the camping idea and not the Christian dimension that attracted our young subject. He and a school friend planned to enjoy the camp, attend a few of the Sunday afternoon Crusader meetings when they got home, and then quietly drop out. They went off to camp as atomic bombs were being dropped and when they returned the war was over. The Japanese had surrendered. While nothing dramatic happened at the camp, except an attack of diarrhea, it set Michael on a path, "which has been the chief way in which my life has gone from that day."

For a year Michael sang in the choir at St. Francis on Sunday morning and then bicycled off in the afternoon to attend a Crusader Bible class. If you were present for ten consecutive meetings, you received a Crusader badge and for fifty weeks, the award was a Crusader Bible. Michael received both, not to mention the 50 pence from the parish choir.

It was a year later at another Crusader camp, that Michael, now fourteen, made the commitment which changed his life. The 150 boys in attendance played lots of ball games and did all the standard camping things, but each evening they sat obediently on narrow wooden benches in a tent lit by smoky hurricane lamps. On August 11, 1946, as dusk was beginning to close in, they sang, "Give me a sight, O Savior."

Michael doesn't remember exactly what the speaker was saying, except that he began to "break through the crust of his adolescent indifference" and he recalls that he felt that the words of the Gospel message were being directed right at him.

He told me of a man who had died for me, who had been weighed down on a cross by my sin, my pride, my disobedience, of a man who had suffered its consequences, felt its guilt, had agonized through it; because that man, who had done it, was the one guiltless, perfect human being, to whom its very presence was exquisite torture spiritually. That man had done it all for me, was offering me forgiveness, cleansing, a new heart, and peace with God and how was I going to respond?

How was Michael going to respond? The choices were clear: gratitude or indifference, hands open to receive an undeserved gift or the clenched fists of rejection. The speaker didn't give an altar call per se, but invited anyone who wished to pursue the matter further to come to his tent after the meeting.

Young Michael wrestled with the idea as he circled the leader's campsite for more than fifteen minutes in ever diminishing concentric circles. Finally he lifted the flap of the tent where, in the half darkness, he discovered the preacher along with twenty to thirty other boys. "There," he recalls, "I made the most serious decision of my life. I, as solemnly as I knew how, invited that man, Jesus of Nazareth, to take me on."

In later years he would fill out the Biblical and theological understanding of the phrase, "Savior of the world." That night "he just took it at face value." Fifty years later he says, "never have I regretted that night's Damascus Road and despite the scores of proper questions that every human being ought to face I have never had cause to doubt its meaning or consequences."

Scripture

Now before faith came, we were imprisoned and guarded under the law until faith could be revealed. Therefore the law was our disciplinarian until Christ came, so that we might be justified by faith. But now that faith has come, we are no longer subject to a disciplinarian, for in Christ Jesus you are all children of God through faith. As many as were baptized into Christ have clothed yourself with Christ. There is no longer Jew or Greek there is no longer male or female, for all of you are one in Christ Jesus and if you belong to Christ, then you are Abraham's offspring, heirs according to the promise.

Galatians 3: 23-29
NRSV

Reflection

There are those who would contend that pressuring adolescents to make religious decisions is unfair and even predatory, that one needs more experience of life before asking for a faith commitment. To such a question Michael retorts, "I can only report what I know to have been true that night. I was conscious, fully conscious, fully conscious that I was facing the first great adult decision of my life and I made it, not, of course, perceiving all the theological nuances and subtleties, but with a mind ice-cold clear that this was the biggest step that I could ever take."

But why should Christians be so shy about sharing their faith with the new generation. One member of my youth group came home at Christmas after her first semester of college and told me about the pressures she encountered at college. "Someone is always trying to get into my mind, my pocket book, or my pants," she said. Should Christians not share?

Hymn

Christ triumphant, ever reigning,
Savior, master, king!
Lord of Heaven, our lives sustaining,
Hear us as we sing.
Yours the glory and the crown
The high renown,
The eternal name.

Word incarnate, truth revealing,
Son of man on earth!
power and majesty concealing
by your humble birth.
Yours the glory and the crown,
The high renown,

The eternal name.

Suffering servant, scorned, ill treated,
victim crucified!
death is through the cross defeated,
sinners justified.
Yours the glory and the crown,
The high renown,
The eternal name.

Priestly King, enthroned for ever
high in heaven above
sin and death and hell shall never
stifle hymns of love.
Yours the glory and the crown,
The high renown,
The eternal name.

So, our hearts and voices raising
through the ages long,
ceaselessly upon you gazing,
this shall be our song.
Yours the glory and the crown,
The high renown,
The eternal name.

Words: Michael Saward, 1964
Words copyright 1966
Jubilate Hymns, Ltd.
Admin. Hope Publishing Co., Carol Stream, Il000 60188

All rights reserved. Used by permission

Chapter Six

The Archbishop's Spouse

Eileen Carey

While it is not in the Guinness Book of Records, Eileen Carey may well be the only woman in the world who has both hugged Billy Graham and kissed the Pope.

The latter occurred when Eileen and her husband were ushered into the private quarters of Pope John Paul II at the Vatican. It was an historic meeting, although there were no reporters or cameras present. As a woman and as the wife of a clergyman she was surprised at the invitation to a private luncheon with the Roman pontiff. After all, her husband was the Archbishop of Canterbury and the first married Archbishop of Canterbury had been declared a heretic and burned at the stake with papal approval in 1556. Eileen was indeed surprised that John Paul II accepted so graciously that George Carey, 103rd occupant of the English Primacy, was a married man. It was more than she had expected from the Vatican. She was also impressed with Karol Jozef Wojtyla the man, "He is a wonderful, charismatic and spiritual man," she told a gathering of the spouses of theological students during a visit to the University of he South, Sewanee, Tennessee. The Pope's spiritual energy radiated through his personality despite his old and frail body. She was so overcome with his persona that at the end of the luncheon, when she and her husband were saying goodbye, "Something came over me and I went and kissed him. He looked so frail He looked as if his robes were too heavy and I just felt that he needed that."

When Eileen was a little girl she had no idea hat she would kiss the pope, be married to the Archbishop of Canterbury, or even be the spouse of a clergyman. All Eileen wanted to do was be a nurse. From the earliest years she can remember, that's what she wanted to be. "I was always putting bandages on my dollies," she recalls. Even going to nursing school was reaching high for Eileen's family. Her father, Douglas Cunningham, had migrated from Scotland to the southeast of England during the depression. He worked for a construction firm as a laborer and raised his family in a modest working class village in Essex. As an infant Eileen was baptized in the local parish church and attended church and Sunday school with her mother and her sister Evelyn. "My father was a staunch believer in and supporter of the Church of England, but he never attended."

When Eileen was in her teens her father, without any explanation to his family, began attending confirmation class and presented himself to the bishop for the laying on of hands. Eileen remembers thinking, "Isn't that nice," but regretfully no one ever asked him why he had done it. From then on Eileen, her father, mother, and sister attended church every Sunday as a family.

"That was a good time for all of us," she recalls. A year later Eileen presented herself for confirmation. She recalls that it was the custom at the time to have a white dress and a veil. She also remembers that she was very well prepared by the vicar who had been in the mission field.. She remembers him as a "very proper Evangelical," who gave them a thorough background and preparation, including stories of missionaries ancient and modern. She became conversant, not only, with the Book of Common Prayer and The Thirty-Nine Articles at the back of the book, but with the Bible as well and was required to commit large portions of scripture to memory. She also learned to listen to sermons about what Jesus had done. She understood that the central part of the Christian faith was Jesus coming into the world, (Incarnation) his death on the cross (Atonement) and his being raised from the dead

(Resurrection). She fell in love with John's Gospel and the Jesus it portrayed. Confirmation was a serious event in Eileen's life and she believed that she was taking the responsibility as an adult for what her godparents had promised for her as an infant at her baptism. She was acknowledging Jesus Christ as her savior and promising to follow him as the Lord of her life. Confirmation for Eileen was more than a white dress and a veil.

When Eileen was sixteen the young American preacher, Billy Graham, was conducting his London Crusade and once a week Eileen and her friends boarded a chartered motor coach that took them to London. The crusade made a major impression on her life as it did on the lives of countless thousands in the United Kingdom. As a teenager she was totally oblivious to the ecclesiastical controversy and power struggle that was going on behind the scenes. Most historians cite the appearance of Geoffrey Fisher, the 99th Archbishop of Canterbury, on the platform as a major turning point, not only for Dr. Graham, but for the future of Christianity in England. Eileen was totally oblivious to all of that. "Archbishops meant nothing to me then, nor did bishops. I hardly knew what they were." Nonetheless, the crusade had its own impact on Eileen.

While Graham concluded each evening with an invitation to come forward and make a commitment, Eileen did not do that. This was in large measure due to the fact that her youth group had been told to get back to the coach as quickly as possible so as not to delay the return journey to Essex. But what Dr. Graham did for her was to "clarify her Christian faith." She believed that she was already a Christian in that she had been brought up in a Christian family and had already made a commitment to Christ and was doing her best to live a Christian life. Graham, had stated the Gospel message in such clear and logical terms that she could accept and affirm it as an adult. The message was simple and the music was moving. She still enjoys "Blessed assurance, Jesus is mine" as it takes her back to that very affirming experience. Eileen's faith became real, serious, and, in fact, her way of life. She discovered the gift and value of having Christian friends; she was excited about the stories told by missionaries and thought seriously about becoming a missionary; and she developed the habit of having a quiet time each day for Bible reading, meditation and prayer. Some forty years later, she notes that she wouldn't want to live her life any other way. "It means so much to me, my faith, I feel I couldn't have coped with all the changes we've had and the sadness we've had in our life without a faith." In the wildest fantasies of her adolescent mind, it never occurred to her that one day she would welcome Billy Graham to Canterbury Cathedral for the enthronement of her husband as the 103rd Archbishop of Canterbury.

It was two years after the Billy Graham Crusade that she met George Leonard Carey, who had just returned from his two years of service with the Royal Air Force in Iraq. Like Eileen, he was from a working class background. He had a job with the London electric company, but was planning to return to school to prepare for the ordained ministry. They met on a bridge as they walked toward a church meeting.

Eileen and George were engaged in 1957. She continued her nurses training and he attended the London College of Divinity. They were married in 1960 as the congregation sang "Oh Praise ye the Lord, Praise him in the height." It has been her favorite hymn ever since and has been played at all of her children's baptisms and weddings. Eileen's nursing paid the bills while her husband completed his theological training. Just before George's ordination in 1962, on April 2, the day after Mothering Sunday, Eileen gave birth to a stillborn 7lb 13oz boy, Stephen Carey. It was a great tragedy for the young couple. Thirty five years later she wrote, "We were both young and getting ready to start our work in a parish in an inner-city deprived part of London, and it was very hard to face this tragic loss and look ahead to the future. With the support of family and friends, and above all the grace and comfort of our Lord Jesus Christ, we slowly began to move forward."

Happily, within the next four years, Eileen, gave birth to a daughter and two sons. Rachel, Mark, and Andrew are all grown now, and have presented their parents with an abundance of grandchildren, but George and Eileen still remember the little fellow who didn't make it. Andrew Carey relates that every year on Stephen's birthday, April 2, his parents go off together. They begin the day by asking each other," Do you know what day this is?" Then they have a prayer and spend a private day together as Eileen and George.

When her husband was offered the position as Archbishop of Canterbury, he was a very junior bishop, having served the Diocese of Bath and Wells for less than three years. In the Church of England bishops are appointed not elected. Technically it is a crown appointment, but before it goes to the Queen for approval, there is a super secret ecclesiastical screening process which brings its findings to the Prime Minister. Recently, the See of Canterbury has alternated between an Anglo-Catholic one time and an Evangelical the next. When Robert Runcie became the 102nd Archbishop of Canterbury, there was also a break with the long standing tradition of elevating the bishops of London, Durham, or the Archbishop of York to the primacy. Runcie had been Bishop of St. Alban's. He had, however, fulfilled an unspoken requirement, that he be an Oxford or Cambridge graduate. George Carey, the first Cockney Archbishop since Becket, was quite a surprise and a major break with tradition.

When George Carey returned from number 10 Downing Street with the invitation in his pocket he announced, "I drew the short straw." The event, Eileen recalls, was "a shock high on the Richter scale." But after some thought and prayer she concluded, "When you know your name's been put forward, you have to ask: is God in this? If you believe that God is in your life, and has been guiding you through the years, then you have to feel very strongly that it's wrong to turn it down."

So, Eileen Carey greets the bishops and spouses arriving at the Lambeth Conference, kisses the Pope, and welcomes Billy Graham to

England. She entertains the Patriarch of Constantinople, attends a state dinner at Windsor Castle, visits with the guests at a homeless shelter for women in central London. She attends daily Morning Prayer in the staff chapel at Lambeth, does her own cooking when she can on weekends, and hangs her laundry on the roof of Lambeth Palace, and with a cheerful smile tells a reporter, "Where I am now is where God wants me to be."

Scripture

In the beginning was the Word, and the word was with God, and the Word was God. He was in the beginning with God. All things came into being through him, and without him not one thing came into being. What has come into being in him was life and the life was the light of all people. The light shines in the darkness, and the darkness did not overcome it.

There was a man sent from God whose name was John. He came as a witness to testify to the light, so that all might believe through him. He himself was not the light, but came to testify to the light. The true light, which enlightens everyone, was coming into the world.

He was in the world and the world came into being through him; yet the world did not know him. He came to what was his own, and his own people did not accept him. But to all who received him, who believed in his name, he gave power to become children of God, who were born, not of blood or of the will of the flesh, or of the will of man, but of God.

And the Word became flesh and lived among us, and we have seen his glory, the glory as of a father's only son, full of Grace and truth.

John 1:1-14
NRSV

Reflection

Becoming a Christian doesn't mean that life is going to be a breeze or without its disappointments or tragedies. What it does mean is that God's grace is going to be available to us if we will but call upon the Lord.

On April 2, when George and Eileen Carey clear their "diaries", and go off by themselves to remember their firstborn son Stephen, the question they ask has a familiar ring to it. "Do you know what day this is?" sounds very much like the query posed by the youngest son at a Hebrew Seder. "Why is this night different from all other nights? As we all know this question is followed by the recounting of the Passover story, God's action in history to liberate the Hebrews from bondage and set them free to serve God as free persons in a new land. Christians discovered that God's action in our lives is called Grace.

Grace is what Eileen and George discovered in the loss of Stephen and in the birth of their three children and many grandchildren. Grace is what Mrs. Carey sensed in John Paul, II and grace is what she heard Billy Graham proclaim. No one could possibly have predicted that the lower middle class couple, who met on a bridge on their way to church back in 1956, would one day occupy Lambeth Palace on the River Thames, but strange things happen when God's grace is let loose in this world.

Eileen's story is by no means trouble free, but it as a very graceful story and she is a very graceful person.

Hymn

> O praise ye the Lord! praise him in the height;
> rejoice in his word, ye angels of light;
> ye heavens adore him by whom ye were made,
> and worship before him in brightness arrayed.

O praise ye the Lord! praise him upon earth,
in tuneful accord, ye sons of new birth;
praise him who hath brought you his grace from above,
praise him who hath taught him to sing of his love.

O praise ye the Lord, all things that give sound;
each jubilant chord re-echo around;
loud organs, his glory forth tell in deep tone,
and, sweet harp, the story of what he hath done.

O praise ye the Lord! thanksgiving and song
to him he outpoured all ages along:
for love in creation, for heaven restored,
for grace for salvation, O praise ye the Lord!

H. W. Baker
Hymns Ancient and Modern #203

Chapter Seven

A Wild Young Man

Billy Graham

They called him Billy Frank, although he was baptized William Franklin Graham, Jr. The world has come to know him simply as Billy Graham.

I first heard of him when I attended a great meeting in Atlanta at the old baseball park on Ponce de Leon Avenue. I was a college student and it was my first experience of a southern revival. It started off with everybody singing a lot of songs I had never heard before, but the tunes were simple; the words were catchy and by the second or third verse my friends and I were singing along in spite of ourselves. George Beverly Shea brought everyone to their feet with the song that would stay with Graham for fifty years: "How Great Thou Art." There were a lot of notable people on the platform. Most of them were pastors at local Baptist or Methodist churches. With much fanfare, the widow of the Reverend Billy Sunday was introduced. She shuffled up to the microphone and said something about the Lord having "anointed Billy Graham to carry on the ministry of my beloved Billy Sunday." There was applause and a few cheers. For some reason, I remember most clearly a Lincoln-esque Methodist minister, Dr. Charles Allen, warming us up for the collection with a few jokes and ending with the request that everyone who had a dollar should wave it over their heads and sing "Bringing in the Sheaves." When a ripple of green waves appeared over the crowd, he commanded, "OK, boys take up the collection." There was laughter and a large collection. A tall gangly young man with wavy blonde hair then seized the pulpit. I don't remember what he said, but he gave the impression of being very intense, that he really believed what he was talking about, and that our lives would be better if we "committed our lives to Christ."

I recall being both moved and intimidated by the whole experience. "Hadn't I already made a commitment of my life to Christ? Wasn't that what confirmation was all about? Hadn't Bishop DeWolfe asked, "Do you promise to follow Jesus Christ as your Lord and savior?" Didn't I reply, "I do!" Wasn't that exactly what the young evangelist was asking us to do? Had I missed something? Had I already been there and done that? And wasn't I already in the process of making a decision to transfer from Georgia Tech to Emory University in order to prepare for the ministry? And yet there was the disappointing memory that the bishop's hands on my adolescent head did not bring on a rush of spiritual ecstasy. There were no skyrockets, nor did the earth move. By the time people were beginning their march "down the sawdust trail," some of them with tears streaming down their face, I wondered if Billy was offering something that I had some how missed six years before at Zion Church, Douglaston. And then there was the unwelcome prospect of facing all those grinning overweight southern preachers who had started clapping their hands and letting go with an occasional, "Amen." I stayed in my seat and slipped out quietly with my friends and headed for the parking lot.

My second vivid recollection of Billy Graham came via the *Los Angeles Times* and Time Magazine. I had deferred my entry into seminary with a three-year tour of duty as an officer in the US Marine Corp. The delay served a dual purpose. I needed time to be sure that I was being called to the ministry of the Episcopal Church and I needed the money that the GI Bill would provide to complete my education. I was stationed in Twenty-nine Palms, California, when I read of Graham's London Crusade. The idea of a southern American evangelist having anything to offer to the spiritual life of the United Kingdom was at first treated as something of a joke. All the stereotypes of revivals, snake handling, and Elmer Gantry style camp meetings were batted about in both the secular and religious press, with the least responsive group being the mainstream Church of England clergy. And yet the reports of massive crowds couldn't be ignored. From the Harringway Arena to White City Stadium to Wembley, crowds were coming night after night. Billy was touching something in the Anglo Saxon spirit which was not being reached by the established church. As noted in Eileen Carey's story, a turning point came when the Most Reverend Geoffrey Fisher, Archbishop of Canterbury, appeared on the platform with Graham on May 22, 1954, and gave the benediction.

Fisher had been under considerable pressure from within and without the church to either endorse or condemn the young evangelist from America. Before going public, he chose to do some personal investigating and invited Ruth and Billy Graham to take tea with him. Billy had never met an archbishop before and was as apprehensive about the meeting as Dr. Fisher.

Ruth Graham soothed her husband's anxieties by suggesting that, "any man who has six sons must be quite ordinary." So, Geoffrey Fisher, wearing gaiters and an infectious smile, welcomed the Grahams to Lambeth Palace. The Grahams found him to be "a charming and delightful man, wholly without pretense, 'who became a great friend.'"

Following the Archbishop's blessing, the stadium sang "To God be the Glory." Grady Wilson, Graham's song leader, was so moved that he threw his arms around Fisher and called him "Brother Archbishop."

Oddly, Edward Carpenter's biography of Geoffrey Fisher makes no mention of the Graham Crusade, although the Archbishop, writing in the Canterbury diocesan newsletter, gave Graham high praise and declared that there was no doubt in his mind that, "the blessing of the Holy Spirit has been upon this campaign." Fisher noted that there was neither "revivalism" nor an exploitation of "emotions," but rather, "a plain delivery of a plain message concerning some of the fundamental Christian truths about God's Gospel and man's need."

My third impression of Billy's ministry came some thirty years later, when my friend Michael Saward and I exchanged parishes "across the pond" for six weeks. He and his wife, Jackie came to Good Samaritan, Orange Park, Florida (my parish in those days) and Lynne and I took up residence in the Vicarage of St. Mary's, Ealing, in the Diocese of London. As we got to know the people of St. Mary's and they began to tell me the stories of their own spiritual journeys, I kept hearing the name of Billy Graham, over and over again. Between the London Crusade of 1954 and his return to Earls Court in 1966, Billy's missions had provided the turning point and/or defining moment for the 30-50 age group who were the leaders of St. Mary's Parish. I had always heard the argument that Graham's approach was emotional, verging on "hell-fire and damnation" and that it couldn't possibly last. But there they were filling up the church every Sunday, serving on the vestry, singing in the choir, teaching Sunday school and giving leadership in their community.

Billy Graham was born on a dairy farm near Charlotte, North Carolina, on November 7, 1918, just four days before the end of World War I. Morrow and William Graham took their first born son to the nearby Associate Reformed Presbyterian Church to be christened William Franklin Graham, Jr. They called him Billy Frank. Almost as soon as he could walk he was doing farm chores. Before daybreak he learned to milk the cows and collect chicken eggs. He loved baseball and dreamed of becoming a professional ball player. His fantasy was encouraged, at age ten, by a handshake from the famous Babe Ruth, although his contemporaries testify that Billy wasn't much more than an average player. His parents took Billy along with his three younger siblings to services and Sunday school at the Presbyterian Church, but he does not remember his parents as being "particularly religious."

By 1933 the Great Depression had rolled over the North Carolina Piedmont. The collapse of the banking system had wiped out all of the Graham's savings. Fortunately, the farm was not mortgaged. But that was threatened by a freak accident when Frank Graham's head was smashed by a flying chunk of wood from a saw mill. The surgeons believed that it would take a miracle to save his life and a local prayer group moved in to support Morrow and her family. Morrow was convinced that the "Lord heard my prayers," and her husband in fact recovered. After that the Graham home life took on a more intense religious flavor, which Billy Frank, age 15, saw as just so much "hogwash." His adolescent spirit found release in sneaking out at night and wildly driving his father's car across the back roads of North Carolina. Suspicious of his son's nocturnal activities, the father began to check to car's odometer and discovered that he added more than 200 miles in one night. Nonetheless, with the energy that only youth can provide, Billy Frank was still faithful in milking the cows before daybreak and doing other farm chores.

At the same time the senior Graham had allowed a tent to be erected in his pasture by a group of Charlotte businessmen who wanted to pray for the city and its recovery from economic and spiritual depression. The farm meeting led in 1934 to an eleven week revival led by the fiery Southern evangelist Mordecai Fowler Ham. It was opposed by the leading clergy of Charlotte, attacked by the press, and attended by the local population.

Ham caught the attention of the local young people when he charged that the local high school was a hotbed of fornication. Infuriated students marched on Ham's makeshift "Tabernacle" and young Billy Frank came out to see what the excitement was all about. He decided that the safest place in the Tabernacle was in the choir behind the podium where he could avoid the "accusatory stare" of the evangelist. Billy Frank sang off key and observed the most exciting show in town. But, little by little Ham's message was getting through to Billy Frank. Writing some 50 years later, Dr. Graham would recall, "What was slowly dawning on me during those weeks was the miserable realization that I did not know Christ for myself. I could not depend on my parents' faith. Christian influence in the home could have a lasting impact on a child's life, but faith could not be passed on nor inherited, like the family silver. It had to be exercised by each individual."

Billy Frank began to suspect that he had fallen into the rut of "rote and ritual" and that his own efforts at "self improvement" were not going all that well. He was in fact bored with his parents' new found piety and did his best to avoid their family gatherings for prayer and Bible reading. Under the pressure of Ham's nightly sermons, Billy Frank pronounced himself "spiritually dead." Then on a November evening close to his sixteenth birthday William Franklin Graham, Jr., responded to the invitation to "accept Christ." In the midst of Ham's tirades against sin, Billy heard the gentler promise, "But God commendeth his love toward us, in that, while we were yet sinners, Christ died for us." (Romans 5:8, KJV) The choir sang four verses of "Just as I am" and then followed it with "Almost persuaded; now to believe, almost persuaded Christ to receive."

On the last verse of the second song, Billy Frank responded. "I walked down to the front," he recalls, "feeling as if I had lead weights attached to my feet, and stood in the space before the platform."

He was one of three or four hundred people who made a commitment that night. He looked around and saw a lady standing next to him with tears running down her cheeks and wondered why he was not crying. He did not feel any special emotion of any kind just then, and wondered whether he was supposed to be there. Was he making a fool of himself? He almost turned around and went back to his seat.

At this point an old family friend put his arms around Billy. There were tears in his eyes and urged Billy to make his decision. He explained to Billy what he needed to do to become a genuine Christian. "The key word," recalls Billy, "was *do*. Those of us standing up front had to decide to *do* something about what we knew before it would take effect"

"Now came the moment to commit myself to Christ. Intellectually, I accepted Christ to the extent that I acknowledged what I knew about Him to be true. That was mental assent. Emotionally, I felt that I wanted to love Him in return for His loving me. But the final issue was whether I would turn myself over to His rule in my life."

No bells went off and there were no flashing lights or rapid heartbeats. He wasn't crying like some of the others around him, but he did feel a gentle peace. His father came up out of the crowd and embraced him and later told him, " Billy, I'm so glad you took the stand you did tonight."

When Billy filled out the card they gave him, he checked "Recommitment." He had been brought up to believe that his baptism and confirmation were professions of faith. But in retrospect he believed that the Ham revival was the moment when he made his "real commitment to Christ," because at that time, at sixteen, he had done it "on purpose " and did it with "intention."

When he went to his room that night, he knelt at the side of his bed for the first time without being told to do so. His prayer was simply," Lord I don't know what happened to me tonight. You know and I thank you for the privilege I've had tonight."

He lay awake in his bed trying to sort it all out. He pictured all of his friends and teachers and wondered who would understand and who would laugh at him or be critical. When sleep came he was still wondering, "What exactly has happened to me?"

When he got up to milk the cows the next morning, "There seemed to be a song in my heart, but it was mixed with a kind of pounding fear as to what might happen when I got to class."

Scripture

For while we were still weak, at the right time Christ died for the ungodly. Indeed, rarely will anyone die for a righteous person-though perhaps for a good person someone might actually dare to die. But God proves his love for us in that while we were yet sinners Christ died for us.

Romans 5:6-8
NRSV

Reflection

Billy Graham's father liked to recall that one of the prayers that was offered by the businessmen in his pasture in 1933 was a prophetic petition to the Almighty by Vernon Patterson, who asked that, "Out of Charlotte, the Lord would raise up someone to preach the Gospel to the ends of the earth." That has certainly happened in the life of the Reverend William Franklin Graham, Jr.

I must confess that it took me quite a while to warm up to and appreciate the ministry of Dr. Graham. When I first went to Atlanta to study architecture at Georgia Tech, I spent my freshman year in culture shock. First I had to learn about grits. Then I discovered that in the South, dancing was a sin. What was going on? I had learned, not only how to dance, but Father Penny had taught me how to jitterbug and do the Lindy Hop at church camp! What was going on? I headed straight for All Saints Episcopal Church on West Peachtree where they fed us a free supper on Sunday night and then put on the records for slow dancing.

When everyone was talking about Billy Graham, one of the sponsors of our college group told about being approached by a co-worker and asked, "Have you been saved?"

She answered, "I was saved when I was baptized; I was saved when I was confirmed; I am saved every time I go to the altar to receive Holy Communion and I was saved two thousand years ago on a cross on a hill outside of Jerusalem."

To which her coworker replied, "That's the trouble with you Episcopalians, you're never sure just when it happened!"

The classical issue here is whether becoming a Christian is a moment in time or a process?

Is salvation something we do for ourselves or is it something God has done for us? In citing Romans 5:8 at a defining moment in his own journey, I believe that Billy Graham would say that, "Yes, salvation is something that we can neither deserve nor earn; it is something that was paid for us at a great price on the cross. It is a free gift, but we must *intentionally* receive the gift and turn over the control of our life to Christ. In Dr. Graham's autobiography *Just as I am*, the chapter detailing his conversion is entitled "The 180 Degree Turn." His decision for Christ meant a new direction for his life and the beginning of a lifetime journey.

When Graham is conducting a crusade and he meets those who have responded to his invitation, his staff tells me that he does not have a "standard" prayer that he says, but that it is fairly close to the following which was recorded at the Ottawa Crusade in 1997.

O God, I am a sinner, I'm sorry for my sin.
I am willing to change my way of living.
Please help me.
I receive Jesus Christ as my savior and Lord.
From this moment on, I want to follow Him.
In Jesus name. Amen.

Hymn

Just as I am, without one plea
but that thy blood was shed for me,
and that thou bidd'st me come to thee,
Lamb of God, I come, I come.

Just as I am, though tossed about
with many a conflict, many a doubt;
fightings and fears within, without,
O Lamb of God, I come, I come.

Just as I am poor, wretched, blind;
sight, riches, healings of the mind,
yea, all I need, in thee to find,
O Lamb of God, I come, I come.

Just as I am: thou wilt receive
Wilt welcome, pardon, cleanse, relieve:
because thy promise I believe,
O Lamb of God, I come, I come.

Just as I am, thy love unknown
has broken every barrier down;
now to be thine , yea, thine alone,
O Lamb of God I come, I come.

Just as I am, of thy great love
the breadth, length, depth, and height to prove,
here for a season, then above:
O Lamb of God, I come, I come.

Charlotte Elliott (1789-1871)
1982 Episcopal Hymnal , #693

Chapter Eight

I Still Like Peanut Butter

Francis Loyo

A film of the 1958 Lambeth Conference showed Anglican bishops from around the world processing into the opening service at Canterbury Cathedral. The group was predominately Caucasian and mainly British. The occasional African or Asian face stood out. In 1968, I observed the line up outside the cathedral. Things were changing. The men at the front of the line, the most junior prelates, were of darker complexion. Only the senior fellows at the end of line were white. Thirty years later the transition was complete. In the "2/3 world" delegations it was Anglo-Saxon faces that were the exception. There were also eleven women bishops, but that's another story. (see Chapter 9)

The African bishops were in many ways the stars of the conference. They arrived with stories of great growth, often achieved under the most difficult of conditions. The country with the largest Anglican population in the world is no longer England but Nigeria. In Africa there is a painful and violent confrontation between the Muslim forces in the north and the expanding Christian population in the south. One bishop told the story of a young man on his was to the bishop's consecration who was captured by the Muslims. They cut off his ear and made him eat it so that he wouldn't, " listen to any more Christian lies" Nowhere is the Christian-Islamic clash more dramatic than in the Sudan.

The first thing I noticed about Bishop Francis Loyo of Rokon in the Sudan was his smile. His teeth were an orthodontist's dream. They went in every possible direction, but there was a charm and a joy in his smile, that I can only describe as winsome. He had only been a bishop for three years and had spent a year of that time in jail. " I asked them, why am I in jail?" said Francis Loyo, with a chuckle and a smile, "and they said I talk too much."

"Talking too much," was the Sudanese government's way of objecting to the formation of Bible study groups and prayer cells, which appear to be the organizational principal undergirding one of most phenomenal examples of church growth in the twentieth century.

The Republic of the Sudan was formed in 1956 after 56 years of Anglo-Egyptian rule. The country covers over one million square miles, making it the largest country on the continent of Africa. It is over 1,400 miles from the Egyptian border in the north to the frontier with Kenya, Uganda, and the Democratic Republic of the Congo on the south. At its widest it is 1,000 miles from Chad, the Central African Republic and Libya on the west, and the Red Sea, Ethiopia, and Eritrea on the east. The population of more than 30 million come from Arabic stock in the arid north to black African people in the south. The northerners speak Arabic and are followers of Islam. The southerners speak English and/or local languages and are either Christians or practice ancient local religions. Anglicans, Presbyterians, and Roman Catholics make up the vast majority of Christians.

Since 1984 the federal government in Khartoum has sought to impose the Arabic language and Islamic law on the country. This has resulted in a civil war which has at times verged on genocide, and has taken as many as a million lives. Against this unstable background the church has operated and even thrived. In 1963 Canon Howard Johnson of New York's Cathedral of St. John the Divine reported, in his book *Anglican Global Odyssey*, that there were 90,000 Anglican Christians in the Sudan. By 1998 the figure had grown to 2,000,000.

Life in the Sudan is very primitive. Most villages lack shops, schools, electricity, and even running water. There are no doctors or medicines. Telephones are non-existent and only footpaths connect neighboring towns. And yet there is a church. Not necessarily a church building, but a community of Christians who gather under a tree or in a grove. Many have walked miles to get there. They sing and praise God and they bring a handful of maize for the offering, which is given to the priest to distribute to the poor and to feed his own family.

When I met with Bishop Francis, he spoke of walking from village to village to make his episcopal visitations. He does not own a bicycle, much less an automobile. "I am fortunate," he says, "God made me simple—and my wife, too. Our needs are simple and God takes care of us."

It follows that Bishop Francis depends on the hospitality of people along the way who feed him, put fresh water in his canteen, and often hide him if there are government troops in the area. He often sings along the road in the Dinka dialect, "Jesus is my friend." He sang it for me and it turned out to be, "What a friend we have in Jesus." Then he adds, " Jesus is my friend—always my best friend." He also reinforces his courage with scripture. His favorite being, " I am the way and the truth and the life." (John 14:6) "Jesus is the way," he says as he smiles. "I need to remember that as I walk along the way. The first Christians were known as people of the way—Jesus' way." When the bishop reaches his destination, it is not unusual for him to baptize and confirm several hundred new Christians. "The church is not growing in riches, but it is growing in the hearts of the people." I could not help but think of Jesus' admonition to the seventy who had been commissioned to go out and announce the "Kingdom."

> *Take no gold, or silver, or copper in your belts, no bag*
> *for your journey or two tunics, or sandals, or a staff; for*
> *laborers deserve their food. Whatever town or village you*
> *enter, find out who in it is worthy, and stay there until you*
> *leave.* (Matthew 10:10-11, NRSV)

How did this man become a Christian? What is the source of his simple faith, lifestyle and his joyful countenance? "I was an orphan," he explains. "I never tasted my mothers milk. I almost died when I was a newborn." Francis, the last of nine children, lost his father shortly after he was born. His mother almost died giving birth, could not nurse her child or care for him. She was an invalid and died two years after Francis was born. Had it not been for his sister Coni, Francis would have perished along with his parents. His earliest memory of his sister was, " I would wake up early in the morning and she would be at my bedside praying. That's when I learned how to pray. It helped a lot because I missed my mother so very much."

When he was a little older, people in the village told him more about his sister Coni and her battle for his survival. Coni took Francis to a Roman Catholic priest for baptism, but what about his physical nourishment? No permanent wet nurse could be found, so Coni went from nursing mother to nursing mother in the village. In exchange for feeding her brother, Coni would agree to prepare a meal for the family. When this was not sufficient she would squeeze the oil out of peanuts or grind the peanuts into a fine powder, mix it with water and place it, drop by drop, on her little brother's tongue. Francis smiles and says, "I still like peanut butter."

When it came time for his education, Francis was taken to Tuba where there was an Anglican Church Missionary Society (CMS) school. He was a bright student and was encouraged to continue beyond the secondary school level. At age twenty, he made a lifetime commitment to Christian service. He apologizes for not "seeing a vision or anything like that. It was more of a, facing of reality—remembering all of the stories of my birth and how my sister and the community had fed me, I said to God, 'all that you have done for me, but what have I done in your service?' That changed my life. I became different."

The local Anglican priest and then the bishop affirmed his call to ministry. Their intent was to send him to the Union Theological

Seminary at the American University in Beirut. However, civil strife in Lebanon made that plan impossible and his education was completed in a local Bible College.

It was time for Bishop Francis to go to a meeting. I mentioned that Hillary Rodham Clinton had written a book, *It Takes a Village*. He smiled and said, "That's true."

Scripture

> *Do not let your hearts be troubled. Believe in God, believe also in me. In my father's house there are many dwelling places. If it were not so, would I have told you that I go to prepare a place for you? and if I go and prepare a place for you, I will come again and take you to myself, so that where I am you may be also. And you know the way to the place where I am going."* Thomas said to him, "Lord we do not know where you are going. How can we know the way?" Jesus said to him, " I am the way, the truth and the life, no one comes to the father except through me. If you know me you know the Father also."*

> John 14: 1-7
> NRSV

Reflection

In the UK, where the bishop's residence is often referred to as a palace, it was difficult to imagine the simplicity of Bishop Francis' life style. And with all due respect to my theological seminary and all of the great books that have been written by theologians, both classical and contemporary, it is refreshing to encounter the simplicity of the faith of the church in the Sudan.

Maybe we Western Christians need to think of ourselves as "people of the Jesus way." So many of the stories coming out of the Sudan tell of Christians willing to die for their faith. It makes me want to ask myself, "For what are you willing to die?" Both Bishop Francis' physical and spiritual life were dependent on others. As Bishop Francis began to hear the story of how his sister and his community had nurtured him, he began to ask himself, "for what purpose was I born; for what purpose has my life been saved? Who were the caregivers in my life? Who are the Christians who saw something of value in me? What can I do in return? What is the purpose of my life?"

Hymn

What a friend we have in Jesus
All our sins and griefs to bear!
What a privilege to carry
Everything to God in prayer!
O what peace we often forfeit,
O what needless pain we bear,
All because we do not carry
Everything to God in prayer!

Have we trials and temptations?
Is there trouble anywhere?
We should never be discouraged:
Take it to the Lord in prayer!
Can we find a friend so faithful,
Who with all our sorrows share?
Jesus knows our every weakness -
Take it to the Lord in prayer!

Are we weak and heavy laden,
Cumbered with a load of care?
Precious Saviour, still our refuge -
Take it to the Lord in prayer!
Do thy friends despise, forsake thee?

Take it to the Lord in prayer!
In his arms he'll take and shield thee,
Thou wilt find a solace there.

Joseph Scriven, 1855

Chapter Nine

Witnessing Heaven Touch Earth

Carolyn Tanner Irish

It was a tense moment for young Carolyn. She had agonized over the issue for days and her whole life depended on the answer she received from the Dean. Less than a year before she had enrolled in the Virginia Theological Seminary and now, depending on the answer she received, she was ready to abandon her studies for the ministry and return to a secular job as a teacher.

"Dean Reid," she asked, "There's something I have to know. Am I a Christian?"

"I've never been asked that question before by a seminary student," mused the Dean. "Is there some kind of a problem?"

The problem came from the fact that Carolyn was born in Utah and she was raised in a Mormon family. While the official title for the Salt Lake City based religious group is The Church of Jesus Christ of the Later Day Saints, the church has many doctrines which are considered unorthodox or even heretical by many mainstream Christian bodies. In many cases, when a LDS member seeks membership in a more traditional church body, they are either re-baptized or baptized conditionally.

Carolyn had never thought of herself as not being a Christian. As a little girl she had learned about Jesus; sung songs about Jesus; colored pictures of Jesus; and heard stories about Jesus. She remembers the LDS church as providing a very special community for children where their talents were valued and put to work. When she was eight years old, the

"Bishop of the Ward" (leader of the parish) called to ask her if she had forgotten to turn in her tithe of 35 cents that week. Carolyn was impressed that the bishop thought that she was important and that her contribution mattered. "I can only imagine what my own children would have said if the rector of the parish had called. It would probably be something like 'get off my back' or 'none of your damn business.'" In retrospect she remembers having a very rich spiritual life, although at the time she didn't "have the words to describe it." She remembers experiencing great "joy and delight in the natural world" but did not associate any of that with God. Religion was confined to what you did in church. The concept that God was the great source of nature would come later in her journey. At seventeen, when Carolyn went off to Stanford University, her father's parting advice had been, "Just stay as near to Jesus as you can."

Carolyn's father, Obert C. Tanner, was both a leader in the Mormon Church and the business and educational life of Salt Lake City. He was one of ten children of a polygamous family that had been abandoned by their father. He had a law degree from Stanford University; was a professor of Philosophy at the University of Utah; had founded a successful business; was a leader in the Mormon Church; and was the author of several books. His Christ, the *Ideal For Living* was used throughout the LDS church for study groups in character development.

Carolyn's mother, Grace Adams, came from the pioneers who migrated to Utah in 1830, under the leadership of Brigham Young. Her great, great, great grandfather, a potter by trade, had been assigned to Parowan, a "Mother Town," in the southern part of the state. The second generation of Adamses became dairy farmers whose "cash crop" was cheese, sold to buyers for the California market.

In her last year of high school Carolyn became an exchange student in New Zealand, which put her in touch with another culture. Her New Zealand "family" were Anglican and she attended the cathedral church in Auckland with her "sister" Jillian. Both young women had work to do on stereotypes. Jillian thought that all Mormons were polygamous and members of a strange sect. While Carolyn looked around the congregation and saw parishioners kneeling and making the sign of the cross and she thought "catholic." Obert Tanner had taken his children to visit non-Mormon churches in Salt Lake City. They had visited Baptist, Methodist, Presbyterian, Lutheran, and Roman Catholic congregations. Somehow they had missed the Episcopal Church. In addition to Sunday services in New Zealand, there were daily chapel services at the school she attended.

When she was nineteen, Carolyn married Leon Irish, a fellow student at Stanford, who had been accepted at the University of Michigan Law School. In Ann Arbor she made Phi Beta Kappa and received a BA degree, with honors in philosophy, while Leon completed his law degree. From Michigan the couple went to England, to Oxford University, where Leon continued his legal studies and Carolyn received an MA in moral philosophy, writing her thesis in the field which is now known as bio-ethics. Oxford also provided her with a second exposure to Anglicanism

In 1968, Carolyn, now pregnant with her first child, and her husband returned to the states and settled in Washington, DC, where Leon began his professional life as a clerk in the Supreme Court and then filled a position in a large DC law firm. Carolyn taught ethics, history, and literature at the Edmund Burke School, a private college preparatory school, and the family grew to include: Stephen, Jessica, Thomas, and Emily. As Leon's law practice became more and more absorbing and demanded more and more travel, Carolyn's religious life found expression in the Washington Friends Meeting House. Those were Vietnam War years, and the Quakers, by definition pacifists, provided a vehicle for her strong anti-war feelings.

But as her family grew, Carolyn started looking for a church where her children could "learn about Jesus." Down by the Potomac River there was a run down little Episcopal church that had been built before the Civil War for the slaves of the old Georgetown families. She tried to drop the children off for Sunday school on her way to the Quaker meeting, but was told by the vicar that Christian education at Grace Church was an intergenerational exercise, and that at least one parent must attend. The Rev. Jo Cowin Tartt further explained that the bishop had been ready to close Grace Church. The riverside area was infested with drugs and crime at night and the membership was down to four little old ladies. "See what you can do," said the bishop, and Father Tartt went to work. He decided that he couldn't compete with the more prosperous Georgetown parishes and so he removed all the pews and advertised Grace Church as a place for "bored Christians and Interested Pagans."

Carolyn found it a perfect place to go on Sunday morning with her small children. Each parent took their turn as a teacher and the congregation would gather around the altar to celebrate the Eucharist. She found the experience very engaging and it was in this place that Carolyn was drawn into "a deeper conversion." Little by little she found herself engaged in the liturgy and realized that she wasn't just there for her children. " I was there for me." Her father's counsel to "stay as near to Jesus as you can," was being fulfilled in this strange place with its liturgy so unlike the order of a LDS service. She was happy with her life. She was not looking for another career path, but then one Sunday morning came "the defining moment" of her life. The preacher was a female seminary student from the Virginia Theological Seminary. Carolyn doesn't remember the scripture that was read or a word of the woman's sermon. She does remember a sense of peace. She suddenly saw herself in the role of a priest and she just couldn't get it out of her mind that that was what she was supposed to be. Carolyn went home and went to her room. She lay on her bed and turned the morning's experience over and over in her mind.

"It was as though you were going down a long corridor with a door at the end; but when you got to the end of the corridor, it was the door on the side that was open. And you didn't know all the time you were walking that the side door was really where you were headed." When she left her room and went downstairs, she knew that she was going to go for Holy Orders or at least offer herself for the ministry of the Episcopal Church. She received a lot of support from both her immediate family and her church community in Washington. When she flew back to Utah to tell her parents of her decision to go to seminary, her father's response was, "Of course!"

Her father, being a professor of philosophy, had taught her to ask questions. Mormonism had nurtured her as a child, but she was an adventurous child and she had many questions to ask. Carolyn honors and values her LDS roots, and never speaks negatively about Mormonism. But as an adult and as a woman she "fought with LDS intellectually" and found it to be "a very small room. It's a very set course and I was an adventurous child and I still am."

So with her family's blessing, Carolyn Tanner Irish enrolled in the Virginia Theological Seminary in Alexandria, Virginia, which brings us back to her appointment with the Dean. He heard her with great patience. She was terrified that he would tell her that she wasn't a Christian. There had always been a question about the Mormons. For Anglican, Roman Catholic, Orthodox, and Protestant churches, the canon of scripture was closed by the fourth century. For the Latter Day Saints, it was reopened in the 19th century to include the Book of Mormon. There were also questions about the Mormon understanding of the Trinity and other traditional church teachings. In the rarefied academic climate of a theological seminary these were issues for late night bull sessions if not classroom debate.

The Dean asked Carolyn if she had been baptized. She remembered it well. She was eight at the time. She was baptized by immersion. That's something you don't forget. She had believed that in presenting herself for baptism, she was committing her life to Jesus Christ.

"Do you remember studying the heresy of the Donatists in the third century?" asked the Dean. The Donatists claimed that sacraments performed by heretical groups or by individuals whose personal life fell short of the Christian ideal were invalid. Augustine of Hippo, among others, prevailed with the argument that baptisms were valid despite any possible wrong thinking or behavior of those performing them.

"Carolyn, when you were baptized," he asked, "were you baptized in the name of the Father and the Son and the Holy Spirit?"

"Yes," was her emphatic answer.

"Then you are a Christian!"

She was overjoyed. The door was now wide open. Had the dean answered otherwise, she believes that she would have had to leave the seminary. "If that had happened," she said, " I would not have had any understanding of grace."

"I rely on grace" she says, and describes her ministry as all about grace, "about Witnessing heaven touch earth—calling people to notice it and live out of it."

Carolyn is now known as the Right Reverend Carolyn Tanner Irish, the tenth Episcopal Bishop of Utah. She was one of eleven women bishops to attend the Lambeth Conference. As she reflected on her spiritual journey she said, "At no point in my life would we ever have seen this trajectory—becoming a bishop in the Episcopal Church. That would not have been anything that anyone would have predicted. But there does seem to be a rightness about it now."

Scripture

You, Lord, you have searched me out and known me;
you know my sitting down and my rising up;
you discern my thoughts from afar.

You trace my journeys and my resting-places
and are acquainted with all my ways.

Indeed, there is not a word on my lips,
…but you, O Lord, know it altogether.

You press upon me behind and before
and lay your hand upon me.

Such knowledge is too wonderful for me;
it is so high that I cannot attain to it.

Where can I go then from your Spirit?
where can I flee from your presence?

If I climb up to heaven, you are there;
if I make the grave my bed, you are there also.

If I take the wings of the morning
and dwell in the uttermost parts of the sea,

Even there your hand will lead me
and your right hand will hold me fast.

If I say, "Surely the darkness will cover me,"
and the light around me turn to night,"

Darkness is not dark to you;
the night is as bright as the day;
darkness and light to you are both alike.

For you yourself create my inmost parts;
you knit me together in my mother's womb.

I will thank you because I am marvelously made;
your works are wonderful, and I know it well.

My body was not hidden from
while I was being made in secret
and woven in the depths of the earth.

Your eyes beheld my limbs, yet unfinished in the womb;
all of them were written in your book;
they were fashioned day by day,
when as yet there was none of them.

How deep I find your thoughts,
O God! how great is the sum of them!

If I were to count them, they would be more in number
than the sand;
to count them all, my life span would need to be like yours.

Psalm 139 1-17
1979 Book of Common Prayer

Reflection

The appearance of eleven female bishops from the US, Canada, and New Zealand at the Lambeth Conference, while noteworthy from an historical point of view, was almost a "non-event" as far as the male bishops were concerned. Although there was some "sword rattling" on the part of a few conservative bishops before the Canterbury gathering, there were no confrontations, no walkouts or angry speeches. The female bishops participated fully in the small Bible Study groups, in committees, and in the plenary debates. All of them made significant contributions to the process. They were photographed by the local paparazzi wherever they went, but as one photographer confided over a Guinness at the local pub, "What's so unusual about a woman in a long purple dress?" The bottom line was that they were welcomed and accepted, and the church moved on with its business.

In Bishop Irish's story, the figure of her father, Obert C. Tanner, stands tall. He reminds me of the great patriarchs of the Hebrew Scriptures who delighted in their children, encouraged them, and gave them their blessing. No one ever becomes a Christian by themselves. There is always someone who tells us the Gospel story; who lives out that story in their own life and encourages us to "stay as near to Jesus as you can."

What is it that we are passing on to our children?

I also was moved by the joy that Bishop Tanner exudes when she is talking about her ministry. I also liked her description of graceful ministry as, "witnessing heaven touch earth—calling people to notice it and live out of it." I think that is one of the best descriptions of grace that I have heard in a long time. What do you think?

Hymn

> I sought the Lord and afterward I knew
> he moved my soul to seek him, seeking me;
> It was not I that found, O Savior true;
> no I was found of thee.
>
> Thou didst reach forth thy hand and mine enfold;
> I walked and sank not on the storm vexed sea;
> T'was not so much that I on thee took hold,

as thou dear Lord, on me.

I find, I walk, I love but oh, the whole
of love is but my answer, Lord to thee;
For thou wert long beforehand with my soul,
always thou lovedst me.

Words: Anon
1982 Episcopal Hymnal, #689

Chapter Ten

On A Pilgrimage To Walsingham

Jonathan David Millard

In the Year of Our Lord 1061, in a remote village of East Anglia on the banks of the river Stiffkey, five years before William the Conqueror defeated England's last Saxon king, a woman named Richeldis de Favaraques (sometimes spelled de Faverches—the people of medieval England were chaotic spellers) had a vision of the Virgin Mary. Jesus' mother appeared asking her to have a chapel built in Walsingham. In her dream or vision Richeldis was taken to Nazareth and shown the *Santa Casa* or Holy House in which Mary had lived and where she was confronted by the Angel Gabriel and told, according to Luke 1:26-38, that she was to be the mother of the Christ Child. Richeldis' assignment was to build a chapel, which was to be an exact reproduction of the room in which the Annunciation took place. The dimensions were specified as 24'6" x 12'10". The Holy House was to contain one door and a small window.

Modern pilgrims to the Holy Land can see the original by visiting the Church of the Annunciation at Nazareth. You go down a flight of stairs to a cave where the words, "Hail Mary full of Grace," were first articulated. I visited the Holy Land site with a busload of pilgrims in 1998. It was quite an experience, especially when two women from my parish joined their voices in chanting the Magnificat, the song that Mary sang when she shared the good news of her pregnancy with her cousin Elizabeth.

My soul magnifies the Lord,
and my spirit rejoices in God my Savior,
for he has looked with favor on
the lowliness of his servant.
Surely, from now on all
generations will call me blessed;
For the mighty one has done great things for me,
and holy is his name.
His mercy is for those who fear him
from generation to generation

He has shown strength with his arm,
he has scattered the proud in the thoughts of their hearts.
He has brought down the powerful from their thrones,
and lifted up the lowly;
He has filled the hungry with good things,
and sent the rich away empty.
He has helped his servant Israel,
in remembrance of his mercy,
According to the promise he made to our ancestors,
Abraham and his descendants forever.

Luke 1:46-55
NRSV

At the time of Richeldis' experience, a spring bubbled up in a nearby field. The appearance of the spring was taken as a sign verifying the truth of Mary's visitation and marked the site on which the shrine was to be built. When the dust had settled after the Norman invasion, the replica of "Our Lady's Home in Nazareth" became the most popular destination for pilgrimages in all England. Eventually an Augustinian Priory was constructed adjacent to the chapel that now sheltered Mary's

House. Its popularity continued even after the shrine of Thomas a Becket was established at Canterbury a century later. Many miracles were claimed by the pilgrims and attributed to the intercessions of the Virgin Mother. The lame walked, the blind received their sight, and lepers were cleansed. An old ballad declared (in Middle English):

> *And syth here our lady hath shewyd many miracle,*
> *Innumerable nowe here for to expresse,*
> *To such as visyte thys hir habytacle,*
> *Ever like newe to them that call hir in dystress.*

Richard the Lion Heart paid a visit after his return from the Crusades. Edward I visited thirteen times and every king and queen of England until the Reformation made at least one visit. Henry VIII made three pilgrimages to Walsingham, paid for many repairs and improvements and sent money twice a year for a candle to be kept burning and for the "wages priest" to say daily mass. That was before Henry's break with Rome and his dissolution order, in 1535, to close down all the country's monastic establishments. Part of Henry VIII's contention was that the religious houses had fallen not only into superstitious practices, but had become centers of immoral behavior. Unfortunately, Walsingham fell into the latter category, with the records of the Diocese of Norwich in 1514 showing an episcopal visit to the Priory which revealed that the Prior himself had a concubine and that he was appropriating to his own use the riches belonging to the shrine.

Students of English history will recall that the religious houses did not disappear quietly and without protest. In October of 1536 there was a Pilgrimage of Grace that rallied 30,000 people at Doncaster to protest the closing of the convents and monasteries. After appearing to be sympathetic to their plea, the king sent an army of foreign mercenaries to put down the revolt. There was also a smaller Walsingham Rebellion, the leaders of which were drawn, hung, beheaded, and quartered. The formal transfer of the Priory took place on August 4, 1538. The celebrated image of Our Lady of Walsingham was taken from the shrine and sent to London where it was publicly burned in Chelsea. By 1539 Henry VIII had taken care of the riches of all the religious establishments of the land and their real estate had been sold at bargain prices to his friends and supporters. Pilgrims to Walsingham, or any other place in England, were no more.

> *Weep, weep, O Walsingham,*
> *Whose days are nightes,*
> *Blessings turned to blasphemies,*
> *Holy deedes to dispites.*
>
> *Sinne is where our Lady sate,*
> *Heaven turned is to helle;*
> *Satan sitte where our Lord did swaye,*
> *Walsingham, oh farewell.*

It was not until the 19th century catholic revival had taken hold within the Church of England that steps were taken to restore the shrine. In their effort to reclaim the ancient catholic heritage of the English speaking people, Our Lady of Walsingham, which dated from Saxon times, was a natural project. To accomplish this the Anglican Society of Our Lady of Walsingham was founded in 1922. At first the parish church of St. Mary housed a statue of the Virgin Mary, but in due time a separate shrine was constructed and pilgrims came from across the British Isles and then from around the world. There is also a Roman Catholic society for the same purpose.

Between the two traditions it is estimated that over 250,000 pilgrims visit Walsingham each year.

Anglican pilgrimages often start in the morning with a celebration of the Eucharist at St. Magnus, London Bridge, before boarding the train for Norfolk. In the afternoon Vespers and Benediction of the Blessed Sacrament at the parish church in Walsingham greeted the pilgrims. Later in the evening, confessions are heard. The second day begins with a High Mass followed by the stations of the cross, the Rosary, visits to the old priory garden, drinking from a holy well, and a walk along the last few miles of the old Pilgrim's Way. It all ends with a procession back to the shrine through the narrow streets of the old village chanting some 38 verses of "The Pilgrim's Hymn" which recounts the shrine's history. Three verses should be enough to give the flavor of the event.

Our Lady, God's Mother in Glory arrayed,
Held a house in her arms which was clearly displayed
Refrain.
Ave,Ave, Ave, Maria! Ave,Ave, Ave Maria!

Take note, my dear daughter, and build here a shrine
As Nazareth's home in this country of thine.
Refrain.

And the spot that I choose where the house shall arise
By a sign shall be plainly revealed to your eyes.
Refrain.

The day ends with sung vespers. A mass on the morning of the third day concludes the exercise. The pilgrims are blessed and sent on their way rejoicing.

Like the pilgrimages of old, many Walsingham miracles are claimed and recorded. From lupus and lameness to laryngitis; from cancer to cataracts; arthritis and angina—the testimonies accumulated.

And not just for medical problems, but spiritual as well. Many conversions are also attributed to a Walsingham visit. On their "weekend off," many people attending the Lambeth Conference ventured north to visit the restored shrine.

While I was reporting the 1998 Lambeth Conference, I met a young man named Jonathan who was working as a steward at the Conference's meeting place—Kent University, near Canterbury. Jonathan's story helped me to understand what Walsingham might mean in the life of a very modern young Brit.

In 1993, Jonathan Millard from Monmouth, Wales, at age thirteen had been, among the Walsingham pilgrims. He was an only child, raised by his mother who earned her living as a child minder (baby sitter in America) and also worked in a day care center. She had Jonathan baptized as a baby and took him to church, and to Sunday school. In due time he became an altar boy and worked his way up to head server and sacristan. But, looking back, he says, "I didn't really become a Christian until I had asked some of the really hard questions about my faith." By age twelve Jonathan was getting bored with church activities and was looking for excuses not to go.

It was at that point in his life that he joined the local pilgrimage to Walsingham. "I was up there," he said, "I was surrounded by a bunch of Christians who were taking it all very seriously. I started asking myself, 'what am I doing here?' I had no idea about what I was supposed to be doing. There I was among a lot of Christians who cared for me. But I seemed to be on the outside, not really understanding what it was all about. I decided that I wanted what they had. I wanted to believe what they believed. I wanted to be a part of the church that they were a part of."

Jonathan sat down with Fr. Chris Nichols at the shrine. "He explained some of the stuff to me," recalls Jonathan. Some of the stuff had to do with the hard questions which, as he recalls the experience, had little to do with Jesus or the Virgin Mary. The primary issue for Jonathan was "What and who is God?" Once he got that straight, Jesus and Mary followed. "God," said Jonathan, "is someone you can trust and is always near you. You can always talk to him. God is everywhere and God is in everyone of us working his way."

He pointed to a group sitting under a tree. "He's in those people over there." Then he looked me straight in the eye. "In your face, I see God!"

Jonathan left Walsingham having vowed to be more devout in his faith and service at his parish church in Wales. But seeing God in the face of others seems to be a recurring theme in Jonathan's life. He likes the passages in scripture about light and darkness. "You can't see in the dark. Only when you're in the light can you see God in other people. A lot of people don't like the light. I have a friend who just came back from El Salvador. He was baptized out there. He said he experienced a soft gentle light, a loving light, which is what God is. He was working in this village and they went to church one Sunday and he said that he was touched by the Holy Spirit. He was touched by light."

Music is also a big part of Jonathan's life. He sings in a choir that toured the U.K. and Europe. He "is keen" on a wide variety of music. He likes Tom Jones and both traditional and contemporary Christian music. Being a Welshman he loves to sing and he loves rugby. The two come together at the beginning of every international match when the stands will ring with the tune *Cwm Rhondda*, which he will gladly render in either English or Welsh.

> *Guide me, O thou great Jehovah,*
> *pilgrim through this barren land,*
> *I am weak, but thou art mighty,*
> *hold me with thy powerful hand.*
> *Bread of Heaven, bread of heaven,*
> *feed me now and evermore*

When I met Jonathan at Canterbury in the summer of 1998 he was one of the many stewards on the Kent campus and was looking forward to entering Oxford University in the fall where he planned to study theology. He is heading for the priesthood, but he plans to take a year off to travel when he graduates from Oxford. Where does he want to go? What does he want to see? "I want to go anywhere and everywhere in the world."

Scripture

And this is the judgment, that light has come into the world, and people loved darkness rather than light, because their deeds were evil. For all who do evil hate the light and do not come to the light so that their deeds may not be exposed. But those who do what is true come to the light, so that it may be clearly seen that their deeds have been done in God.

John 3:19-21.
NRSV

Reflection

While it was Chaucer who wrote of the frivolous side of a holy pilgrimage in his *Canterbury Tales,* it was John Bunyan who likened the Christian life to a pilgrimage; a journey toward a holy place with many distractions, diversions, and obstacles. I came away from my visit with Jonathan with the strong sense that he was indeed a pilgrim. Like Bunyan's Pilgrim he was being drawn gently and firmly away from darkness into light. He was a work in progress; a young man definitely on a journey. And like the travelers in Chaucer, his infectious laughter exposed the fact that he was enjoying the trip. The journey began with Jonathan's baptism as an infant. Dr. George Carey, the 103th Archbishop of Canterbury has said of infant baptism, "The church included me in before I included myself in. I think that there's something very very significant theologically about the generosity of a church which is prepared to take risks."

When young Jonathan journeyed to Walsingham he was surrounded by a group of people whom he admired, loved, and trusted and who appeared to have something that he didn't. When Jonathan vowed to be more faithful he was responding to his baptism and he began the process of "including himself in." At age eighteen, when I met Jonathan, he was just beginning his pilgrimage. He had chosen to walk toward the light. For those who can identify with any or all of this story, it might be good to reflect on your own journey. In what direction am I moving? Where am I in my pilgrimage?

Hymn

> *Who would true valour see,*
> *let him come hither;*
> *one here will constant be,*
> *come wind come weather;*
> *there's no discouragement*
> *shall make him once relent*
> *his first avowed intent*
> *to be a pilgrim.*
>
> *Whoso beset him round*
> *with dismal stories,*
> *do but themselves confound;*
> *his strength the more is.*
> *No lion can him fright;*
> *he'll with a giant fight,*
> *but he will have the right*
> *to be a pilgrim.*
>
> *No goblin nor foul fiend*
> *can daunt his spirit;*

he knows he at the end
shall life inherit.
Then, fancies, fly away;
he'll not fear what men say;
he'll labor night and day
to be a pilgrim

John Bunyan (1628-88)
Hymns Ancient and Modern #212

Chapter Eleven

A Prince In The Rain And A Bomb On The Roof

Louis Tsui

When I think of Hong Kong, I think of the Prince of Wales, on July 1, 1997, dressed in full military gear, standing at attention in the pouring rain as the Union Jack was lowered and fire works were ignited to mark the end of 155 years of British rule and Hong Kong's return to the government of China.

Louis Tsui's (Pronounced Sue) earliest memory of Hong Kong was living in an apartment with an unexploded bomb on the roof and soldiers out in the streets. That was back during the dark days of World War II. The bomb came from the British or Americans. The soldiers were part of the Japanese Army that had swept through the Philippines and the China Sea following their attack on Pearl Harbor on December 7, 1941.

"Don't go out on the street and don't go up on the roof," he was instructed by his mother. As a little boy during the war his play areas were definitely limited. When the war was over Louis remembers the demolition team that came to take the bomb away. The four story apartment building was cleared of all it occupants as the British soldiers climbed five flights of stairs to the roof. The children stood at a safe distance down the street and waited and prayed until the deadly explosive was gently loaded into the back of a lorry and whisked away.

The third floor flat that was occupied by the Tsui family during the war years was a Christian household. Louis' parents and grandparents were Christians. In a strange way the bomb on the roof played a major role in Louis' faith formation. " The bomb sat on the roof and didn't explode. It fell but it did not explode." he said. " That's why I'm always thankful for life. If it explode, I do not exist."

Before the war Louis' father had been a clerk for a British shipping and trading company, but during the occupation all he could get were odd jobs. Food was expensive and rationed and they lived in fear of the Japanese soldiers who were known to shoot people on the streets. When the war ended the Americans brought in food, but they were still poor and Louis did not start school until he was seven.

The nearby St. Mary's Anglican Church was a major factor in Louis' life. He attended Sunday school, sang in the choir, and participated in the youth group. Following confirmation he went through a period of doubting and searching. Only 10% of Hong Kong's 3 million inhabitants were Christians, and the Anglicans were a mere 5% of that number. (The population is now around 7 million, but the percentages remain the same.) Young Louis wanted to know more about "other ways." Buddhism, Taoism, and Confucianism were the major Asian religious competitors. Communism had already taken over mainland China, and so Louis tried to understand the teachings of Karl Marx as well as the workings of capitalism. Louis smiled and giggled a bit when he said, "Confirmation is supposed to come at the end of the search for identity; for me it was the beginning. There was a hunger in me. I go and then I come back to the Anglican Church—that's where I had a sense of belonging. I liked the liturgy and the fellowship, and that's where I felt empowered, where my self image was built."

When he came back, Louis was ready for college and enrolled in an Anglican school, St. Paul's College, Hong Kong. This also coincided with a serious consideration of the priesthood as his vocation. "My teacher in school advised that I should think and pray about it."

About that time an American clergyman, the Rev. Canon Howard A. Johnson, visited Hong collecting material for his 1964 book, *Global*

Odyssey. He described the state of the church in Hong Kong as a "Full time job by part time priests." As for Christians on the mainland he was advised, "If you have a Christian friend, do not send him as much as a postcard. The only outward way in which you can now express love is by leaving him severely alone."

Against this background, Louis Tsui, at age 17, visited the Bishop of Hong Kong, "to seek his advise and ask for guidance." The advise he got was that due "to the uncertainty in the world and in the church that I study other subjects before theology. I should strengthen other subjects so that if anything happen to the priesthood and the church, I would have another profession to go into and make a living." Louis laughed again, "When I went to see the bishop the future of the church in Hong Kong didn't look too bright. But the bishop said, 'Go on!'"

And "go on" he did: first to the University of Hong Kong, where he became a tutor in history. Then on a world educational tour with stops at the University of Georgia, in Wales, and Toronto. He had acquired a wife and more degrees that a thermometer, including a Master of Divinity with honors from the University of Toronto. Then he wrote the bishop, "I'm coming home."

This was something of a surprise to Bishop Baker who thought that Louis, like so many other men of his generation, would find the political and economic security of the West too appealing to return to Hong Kong. Furthermore, Louis had no financial obligation to return. He had worked his way through his education, either as a tutor, lecturer, shopkeeper, waiter, or dishwasher. When Louis did return and was ordained in 1978, the bishop told him, "I thought you would not be coming back." In 1995 he was consecrated a bishop and is responsible for the Kowloon (mainland) area of the Hong Kong Diocese. His strong academic background plus his love for people and their pastoral care makes him a natural for a diocese in which there are 45 kindergartens, 48 primary schools, 33 secondary schools, one college, and 75 social service agencies. There are only 47 congregations in the diocese serving

29,000 baptized persons, but with the outreach of the schools and agencies, Bishop Louis Tsui estimates that as many as one third of the people in Hong Kong are touched in some way by the Anglican Church. "This is a great opportunity for evangelization," he says.

With the image of the rain dripping from Prince Charles' cap still in my mind, I wondered how things had gone since the transfer of power? Bishop Tsiu was optimistic. At first many people with British citizenship left, but many are coming back. "The political situation is stable. They (the mainland government) promised 'one nation two systems' and life goes on as usual. All the former systems are there. The civil servants are there. All the top officials are there." As for the church, it has undergone changes and is growing. In the past Anglicanism was regarded as a foreign religion and was in fact very British. During the period of China's isolation, the remnants of the mainstream churches on the mainland developed, at the government's insistence, the "The Three Self Church," a government sanctioned union of the former Anglican and Protestant churches. Many Chinese leaders blamed the Western denominational missionaries for inviting foreign powers and influence into China. "But the church is now Chinese as well as Christian and it belongs to the people and to the Lord."

So much for the prince in the rain. As for the bomb on the roof, Bishop Tsui reiterates, "I'm always thankful for life. If it explode, I do not exist."

Hong Kong was the place where, in 1943, the first woman priest in the Anglican Communion was ordained. Her name was Li Kim Oi and she lived well into her eighties. At the time her ordination was regarded as "a wartime exception," but the exception has now become the rule and three of the 48 active clergy in the diocese are female.

Scripture

Truly, I tell you, just as you did it to one of the least of these, who are members of my family, you did it to me.

Matthew 25:40
NRSV

Reflection

The gift of life! What a beautiful gift it is and how lightly we regard it. "Why was I born, and for what purpose have I been given the gift of life?" is a question every human being needs to ask. When one's life has been spared from a bomb on the roof or a childhood disease, the question is even more compelling. Did God put me here for a purpose or am I just an accident?

Bishop Tsui's story also underlines the critical role the Christian family plays in faith development. To be nurtured by two people who have Christ at the center of their life is a priceless gift. To have a community of Christians as an extended family is the place where one has a sense of belonging; where one's self image is shaped and empowered. The church is the home base to which one returns when one's curiosity about other faiths has been satisfied.

There is also something to be said for the Christian family that knows that it is a minority. "We are not like other people. We are Christians," says the parent, "and despite what the neighbors are doing or saying, this is what Christians do and believe." Such a stance may be rough at times, but I believe the long range effect is very positive. The door is always open to the person without the nurturing of a Christian family, but God bless the Christian family. What do you think?

Hymn

The Church's one foundation
Is Jesus Christ her Lord;
She is his new creation
By water and the word:
From heaven he came and sought her
To be his holy bride;
With his own blood he bought her
And for her life he died.

Elect from every nation,
Yet one o'er all the earth,
Her charter of salvation,
One Lord, one faith, one birth;
One holy name she blesses,
Partakes one holy food,
And to one hope she presses,
With every grace endued.

Though with a scornful wonder
Men see her sore oppressed,
By schisms rent asunder,
By heresies distressed;
Yet saints their watch are keeping,
Their cry goes up, "How long?"
And soon the night of weeping
Shall be the morn of song.

Mid toil and tribulation,
And tumult of her war,
She waits the consummation

Of peace for evermore;
Till with the vision glorious
Her longing eyes are blest,
And the great Church victorious
Shall be the Church at rest.

Yet she on earth hath union
with God the Three in One,
And mystic sweet communion
with those whose rest is won.
O happy ones and holy!
Lord give us grace that we
Like them, the meek and lowly,
On high may dwell with thee.

Samuel John Stone (1839-1900)
1982 Episcopal Hymnal, #525

Chapter Twelve

How Could Something So Bad Be Called Good?

Mother Rosina

There was a great mystery concerning the death of Eric. To begin with a little girl that no one had ever seen before or since, came running into the village crying, "Eric has drowned, Eric has downed!" How did the little girl know his name? Where did she go after she announced his death? Why was his body recovered several days later one mile *up stream*. There is an old African saying that the sea is a place for life, not death, so the sea sends dead bodies back to land. It puts them back on the beach. But the stream flows into the sea. How did Eric's body come ashore upstream? And if he drowned, how come his arms and legs were broken?

There was a mystery and also a crisis of deep spiritual dimensions which were activated by Eric's death. Eric was Rosina's only surviving son. She had experienced nine miscarriages. Twin girls had died at birth due to mistakes made by a midwife at the hospital who refused to call in a physician. Then there was Eric, a brilliant young man who had just won a scholarship to Cambridge. When Rosina received word that Eric was missing she caught the first plane back from the United States to Africa. Her faith, which crystallized when she was only four and a half years old, faced its greatest test.

When Rosina was a little girl she had lived in a gold mining town in Ghana on the west coast of Africa. Ghana was still a British Colony when World War II ended in 1945. Her father was the principal of a Church of England mission school and she grew up in a Christian home. Her parents said prayers with her in the morning and the evening and told her Bible stories. "I don't ever remember a time when I wasn't a Christian. Dad and Mom prayed all the time," says Rosina. As soon a she was able to walk, she was taken to Sunday school. "I loved to sing the songs and hear the Bible stories of Jesus and the Hebrew children," she says. "And when I found out that there was a book called the Bible that had all the stories in it, I wanted to have that book so that I could read the stories for myself. It was like discovering a treasure."

When she was not quite five she came home from Sunday school in tears. It was Palm Sunday and the teacher had told the children all about the parade and the palm branches and how everybody was happy to see Jesus. Rosina liked that because she loved Jesus and wanted to join the parade. When the teacher mentioned, almost in passing, that on Good Friday they were going to kill Jesus, she was shocked. "How could they do such an evil thing and call it good?" thought Rosina. "Why did they have to kill Jesus?" She started to cry. "Why did they have to kill him? Why did they have to kill a mother's only son?" Even at four and a half, her sense of fairness was insulted. "What was good about killing someone's child?" The teacher tried to explain, but the harder she tried, the more Rosina cried. To make matters worse, the teacher tried to explain that it was called Good Friday because Moses taught, "an eye for an eye and a tooth for a tooth," but Jesus had taught that if someone hits you that, "you turn the other cheek."

"Well," retorted little Rosina, "if that's what Jesus said, I don't like him; I like Moses better." Even then she had a sense of justice, a concern for someone who was treated unfairly. At that point in her life, an eye for an eye made more sense than turning the other cheek. She ran home to her father sobbing, "Why did they have to kill Jesus?"

Her father took the little girl in his arms, sat her on his lap, and tried to explain. She still remembers that he told her, "God loves all the children in the world just like me, and the Hebrew children, and all the other children in the world. When God created us something happened and we lost the way back to God and so God sent Jesus to come into our life so that he could bring us back to God."

"I heard that," says Rosina, "and because God loves us so much he doesn't want us to get lost forever, he sent his son so that we could all come home to God." Rosina looked at her father and from the look on his face believed that he was telling the truth. "I could see in his face the genuineness of what he was telling me."

"So, it means that God loves me?" Rosina asked her father as he wiped away her tears.

"Yes!"

"And Jesus loves me enough to die for me? she continued.

Her father nodded in the affirmative, "Yes!

"And that's why God sent Jesus to us?"

"Yes!"

"If that's so," declared the little girl, "I'm going to love him back."

Rosina recalls a home in which there was a small chapel where the Bible was read and prayers said every day. In addition to being the principal of St. Paul's Anglican School, her father was the organist at the church. She therefore received a very thorough Christian education in the Anglican tradition.

Eight days after she was born, it was the custom in her village to hold a naming ceremony. At daybreak the extended family gathered in her parents' house. Thanks was given for the safe delivery and then a libation was poured out on the ground to the ancestors. This was not a church ritual, but a family and tribal community rite. Rosina was welcomed into this world from the spirit world and the family as extended family takes responsibility for sharing in the child's upbringing. " The family members are the child's baby sitters, so the child grows up knowing how to socialize with different members of the family," states Rosina.

The custom in Ghana today is to baptize children of Christian families shortly after their birth. Rosina has no idea why her parents waited until she was seven. "All I can guess," she says, "was that they wanted to be sure we at least understand a little about God before we make that commitment." She was seven when she was baptized and remembers very clearly the event and the priest who told her that God had something very special in mind for her life. Rosina knew exactly what that was. She had known as early as her Palm Sunday experience that someday she was going to be a priest. And her resolution was made long before women were being ordained to the priesthood anywhere in the Anglican Communion.

That was an early premonition, but not the only one she ever had. She once told her father that she had a dream about an auto accident in which a relative was killed. When the accident occurred just as she had described it, her father told her not to tell anyone because, "They'll think you're strange."

Now in her fifties, Rosina reports, she has never diverted from that belief. " It was something so deep seated . For me, becoming a Christian was not being converted from one thing to another. He's always been in my life." The knowledge of God that was planted in her heart as a child, was a God of love. "I was given a picture of a loving God that I can trust, believe in, depend on, no matter what I do. This God loves me and provides for my needs." Nevertheless, her life has not been without its pain, nor her faith without its crosses.

When Rosina was eighteen she was married to one of her brother's friends. Many advised against the union, because they were of different tribes. But the wedding took place anyway. Rosina was presented with the traditional gifts. The groom presented her with a large chest, filled with linens and clothing for her new home and clothes for the children she would bear. In recalling her miscarriages, she identified with Hannah, the mother of Samuel in the Old Testament (1 Samuel 1:1-27) Like Hannah, she wept at the altar, pleading with God for the gift of a child. Eric was the answer to her prayer, "Eric became to me like Hannah's son, Samuel—born out of pain and frustration." Three years later she almost died delivering twin girls who were dead on arrival, strangled by their own umbilical cords. "They shouldn't have died," states Rosina, "They should have lived. The midwife at the hospital didn't know what she was doing. She could have called a doctor, but she didn't."

The death of her twins and her own brush with death left her afraid of additional pregnancies. "My in-laws were not happy with my not having more babies. In Ghanaian culture, it is traditional for families to have more than just one or two children." Her in-laws, who had advised against the marriage at the beginning, now advised their son, "Get a wife of your own tribe who can give you healthy children." Eventually the marriage was dissolved and Rosina struggled to raise her only son as best she could. This included heavy physical work at a glass factory lifting 120 pound bags of chemicals. Later she became a full time business woman , "buying foodstuffs from the villages and selling them in the market in the cities. I also baked bread and cakes and sold them in the evenings in the cinema halls."

As Eric grew into manhood, the vocation to priesthood reasserted itself in his mother. The Anglican Church in Ghana had a strong Anglo-Catholic tradition inherited from the missionary work of the old Society for the Propagation of the Gospel (SPG). Rosina, therefore, was familiar with the work of the religious orders in her country and came in contact with the Sisters of St. Helena, who at the time were working closely with the Holy Cross Fathers in a ministry to lepers.

Maybe her sense of vocation to ministry could be fulfilled as a sister in a religious order. Would they accept a married and divorced woman? The answer was not an easy yes or no, but it would be possible when Eric reached his eighteenth birthday. Eric was a good student—brilliant according to his mother's estimate and all sorts of scholarships were offered to him. On Eric's eighteenth birthday, Rosina began a new chapter in her spiritual journey and came to the United States to join the

Order of St. Helena. The sisters, not only received Rosina, but discovered her own brilliance and encouraged her to follow a course of study which would lead to the priesthood. It was in this context that she received the news of Eric's disappearance and death.

The broken limbs were never explained; the crime never solved. The questions of that long ago Palm Sunday reasserted themselves. How could something so bad be called good? Rosina's only consolation was in the knowledge that Mary also knew the pain of losing her only son."

Rosina is now the Reverend Mother Rosina Ampah, OSH. She was ordained a priest in 1993 and now is head of the Order of St. Helena. I wanted to say that she's the mother superior of the order, but no one is superior to anyone else in the order. She is one of four sisters who "share the leadership responsibility." I first met her at the altar at the daily Eucharist at Lambeth. She was distributing the Communion wine and the loving glow on her face and the sparkle in her eyes made me want to know her better and hear her story. She was one of many, many members of religious orders throughout the Anglican Communion who had volunteered to maintain a prayer chapel in the Senate Building on the Kent University Campus.

"I wanted so much to be a mother," she said. "I was created by God to be a mother, but not the way I expected." God, she contends, is always sending her children. She referred to Victor, a friend of Eric's, who embraced her at Eric's funeral and told her, "I will be your son. You will be my mother." Her identification with Mary was complete. "Woman behold your son. Son behold your mother." (John 19:26-7)

Scripture

As she continued praying before the Lord, Eli observed her mouth. Hannah was praying silently, only her lips moved, but her voice was not heard; therefore Eli thought she was drunk. So Eli said to her "How long will you make a drunken spectacle of yourself? Put away your wine." But Hannah answered, ", "No, my lord, I am a woman deeply troubled ; I have drunk neither wine nor strong drink, but I have been pouring out my soul before the Lord. Do not regard your servant as a worthless woman, for I have been speaking out of my great anxiety and vexation all this time. Then Eli answered, "Go in peace; The God of Israel grant the petition you have made to him."

1 Samuel 1:12-17
NRSV

Reflection

There was so much joy radiating from Rosina's face when she gave me communion that I wanted to know more about her. Why am I always surprised when I discover that Christian joy is so often preceded by great pain and difficulty? But isn't that experience at the very heart of the Gospel? Was it not Jesus who, "went not up to joy but first he suffered pain and entered not into glory before he was crucified?" (Collect for Monday in Holy Week, BCP p.220) Rosina's joy and strength came not from having had an easy life, but in discovering that the Hebrew children and Jesus and his followers had not had an easy life, but had discovered a God of grace. I believe that it was Bishop John Coburn, former Diocesan of Massachusetts, who observed that becoming a Christian has to do with discovering the points at which the Bible story and our own story intersect. This idea is certainly illustrated in Rosina's identification with Hannah and Mary and is reflected in the choice of the hymn that follows.

A good question for the reader to ponder might be what is my story and where does it connect with Jesus' story?

Hymn

Lord, it belongs not in my care
whether I die or live:
to love and serve thee is my share,
and this thy grace must give.

Christ leads me through no darker rooms
than he went through before;
he that unto God's kingdom comes
must enter by this door.

Come, Lord, when grace had made me meet
thy blessed face to see;
for if thy work on earth be sweet,
what will thy glory be!

Then I shall add my sad complaints
and weary sinful days,
and with the triumphant saints
that sing my Saviour's praise.

My knowledge of that life is small,
the eye of faith is dim;
but 'tis enough that Christ knows all,
and I shall be with him.

Richard Baxter (1615-91)
Hymns Ancient and Modern, #242

Chapter Thirteen

I Have Always Been A Christian

Satoshi Kobayashi

The date was August, 6, 1998. On the church calendar it was the Feast of the Transfiguration. By secular reckoning it was the 53rd anniversary of the dropping of the atomic bomb on Hiroshima.

At the Lambeth Conference, each of the Provinces of the Communion had been given responsibility for a morning or evening service during the three week gathering. Each day was a unique experience and celebration of both the unity of the church in Christ and its great diversity as the Anglican liturgy had been translated into languages "understanded of the people" and transposed into cultural expressions which were not even remotely British.

The assignment of August 6 to the Japanese Church, the Nippon Sei Ko Kai, had an unsettling note about it. The Americans prepared themselves for a guilt trip about the atomic bombs dropped on Japan at the end of the war. What they experienced was something quite different and very reconciling.

As worshippers entered the great tent where the Eucharist was to be celebrated, they were handed a copy of a statement issued by the Japanese Church. It acknowledged the suffering inflicted by Japan during the war and apologized for their support of the Imperial government at that time.

A moving sermon was preached by the Canon Susan Cole-King who was touched deeply by the statement because, "my father was one of the many Japanese prisoners of war who suffered from the atrocities perpetrated by their captors."

She related that her father, Leonard Wilson, struggled with bitterness and hatred and Christ's command to love our enemies. In prayer he was given a vision of his cruel torturers, "as they might have been as little children, and its hard to hate little children." After the war Leonard Wilson became Bishop of Singapore and "had the great joy of confirming one of his Japanese torturers."

As for "the bomb," she deeply mourned the Japanese lives lost and the suffering inflicted at Hiroshima and Nagasaki and prayed that, "men and women of the world would never again plan war." As one who attended the service, I can testify to the fact that the exchange of the peace that followed was the most meaningful I have ever experienced.

Later that morning, I met with Barnabas, a steward at the Conference. He also had a Japanese name, Satoshi Kobayashi, but insisted on identifying himself by his Christian name. Who gave him that name? "My parents and grandparents and godparents when I was baptized." The conversation was beginning to sound like a page out of the old catechism and I wanted to add, "wherein I was made a child of God and an inheritor of the kingdom of Heaven." I recited those words to Barnabas, and he nodded his head in approval.

Barnabas also approved of what had happened that morning at the Eucharist. "Reconciliation is important." He agreed with Canon Cole-King's statement that "unconditional forgiveness, true reconciliation, can only happen when there is an acknowledgment of wrongs done, when the truth is faced, and painful self-examination leads to confession and apology."

Barnabas identified himself as a fourth generation Christian. His great grandfather had gone to the United States in the nineteenth century and had become a Christian and then came back to Kyoto, Japan. His grandmother and grandfather were both Christians and his mother told him that during the war the Japanese Christians were persecuted by "special police." He remembers as an adolescent picking up an old Japanese Book of Common Prayer and reading the prayers for the Emperor. "How could they pray such a prayer when so many evil things were being done in the name of the Emperor." As a young man in his twenties, he was happy when the Nippon Sei Ko Kwai, "took responsibility for the war and apologized."

As for his personal faith, Barnabas said, "I did not convert. I have always been a Christian." He was baptized as an infant and then presented for confirmation as an adolescent. Confirmation was a major event in his life. "It was important for me because it was important for me to have an initiation. I wanted to follow Jesus and I wanted to work for the church." He credits the "strong influence from his parents" and especially his mother and her very strong faith.

His mother said prayers with him, read and told him Bible stories, and sang simple Christian songs to him when he was a child. And then there was their strong example. "I really came to know Jesus as servant through their strong behavior."

The concept of servanthood was a major theme in our conversation. He is a deacon and does not aspire to be a priest. "My purpose is to follow Jesus as a servant and to help our church follow Jesus as a servant community." For Barnabas, a key word in the scripture is "repent."

"It doesn't just mean to be sorry for your sins, or to be converted or to turn around. The Greek word *metanoia* means to stand in a different place and to look at things from a different point of view. Christians are called to stand where Jesus stood with the poor and the helpless and to see what he saw. Our point of view needs to move to a place where we can think about oppressed people."

That seemed like a good place to end our conversation. Barnabas had to report for duty in ten minutes. We exchanged the peace and went our separate ways.

Scripture

Now, after John was arrested, Jesus came to Galilee, proclaiming the good news of God, and saying, "The time is fulfilled, and the kingdom of God has come near, repent and believe in the good news."

Mark 1:14-15
NRSV

Reflection

The word *metanoia* is a key word in understanding how one becomes a Christian. It is most often translated as *repent* and means to have a change of mind or a change of direction. But Barnabas, without violating the original Greek word, had added a new dimension to the familiar word. I found it rather ironic that a Japanese deacon would help an American understand the meaning of a Greek word. Repentance as standing in a new place; where had I heard that idea before? I mean the idea of standing where Jesus stood and seeing what Jesus saw. Did it come from a visit to the Holy Land? Is that what I felt when our group stood on the Mount of Beatitudes and looked over the Sea of Galilee. That was close. Even closer was walking the Way of the Cross through the narrow lanes of the Old City of Jerusalem. But that wasn't it either. Then I remembered. John Cowling, a friend I met at a communication conference, introduced me to the work of the Christian TV Center near St. Albans, north of London.

CTVC occupies one of the old J. Arthur Rank film studios and produces religious documentaries for British and sometimes American TV. When I visited their operation in the early 90's, they had just completed "Jesus Christ Movie Star." The title was an obvious play of words on Andrew Lloyd Webber's "Jesus Christ Superstar." It chronicled over 100 years of the film industry's attempts to portray the New Testament story in film. Long before Cecil B. De Mille's *King of Kings*, the silent stars were walking on water, feeding the five thousand, and dining in the Upper Room. After a decade of use and abuse, the British Government attempted to regulate the new industry by creating the British Board of Censors which, in 1913, decreed that (1) there would be no scenes depicting frontal nudity and (2) there would be no pictures of Jesus' face. He could be viewed from the back, or the camera could focus on what he was looking at. I'm sure there were a dozen practical reasons for the regulation, but I was struck at the time of the profound theological implications of seeing the world through Jesus' eyes! Is that not what we are invited to do when we read the Gospels? I can only say "Amen" to Barnabas' interpretation of *Repent*.

Help us Lord to see what you see and to do what you would do.

Hymn

O gracious light, Lord Jesus Christ,
in you the Father's glory shone.
Immortal, holy, blest is he,
and blest are you his holy Son.

Now sunset comes, but light comes forth,
the lamps are lit to pierce the night.
Praise Father, Son and Spirit:
God who dwells in the eternal light.

Worthy are you of endless praise,
O Son of God, Life giving Lord;
Wherefore you are through all the earth
and in the highest heaven adored.

Third Century Canticle
1982 Episcopal Hymnal, # 25

Chapter Fourteen

Christ Became My Christ

Elizabeth Whiting Chance

When Libby was only three she almost died of croup. Her mother, who almost never left her with a baby sitter, had on a rare occasion gone out for the evening. A sniffle and an occasional sneeze became a cough and then turned into wheezing. When Libby's parents came home she was gasping for breath. Her esophagus had all but closed. Her father, an opthamologist, rushed her to the local hospital. For a while they thought they might have to do an emergency tracheotomy on her tiny wind pipe. As her mother held her in her arms, rocked her and soothed the frightened little girl, she recited the 23rd Psalm. The part that Libby, Elizabeth Whiting Chance, remembers best was, " Yea though I walk through the valley of the shadow of death, I will fear no evil, for thou art with me." When she learned to read, she was given a book, *Little Visits from God,* that included the 23rd Psalm. She memorized it and recited it as a surprise for Tilly, her great grandmother.

Libby is from Moorhead City, North Carolina, and is one of those fortunate individuals who grew up in a Christian home. She was baptized as an infant, attended Sunday school, sang in the choir, and became part of the youth group. When I met her she was eighteen and working as a volunteer at the Lambeth Conference. Running errands, delivering messages, handing out programs, guarding doors, clearing tables, whatever needed to be done, Libby and her coworkers did it.

Libby realized that this was no ordinary gathering of ordinary men and women. On the first day in Canterbury she heard that a certain

African bishop would be unable to attend because he had been shot. On another occasion she had to track down a bishop to tell him that one of his priests had been kidnapped. She heard tales of horror from the civil war and genocide in Rwanda and persecution and sacrifice from India and Pakistan.

When a group of British and North American stewards decided to skip the university cafeteria food and venture into Canterbury for a night on the town, they invited their third world colleagues to join them. "Will dinner cost more than five pounds?" was the question posed by an African steward. "Probably ten pounds ($16.50) at least," was the American reply. The African declined, explaining that he could feed his family for a week on that amount of money.

"You look at the world and you look at your problems." reflected Libby. "Should I eat that because it's too fattening, or should I wear a blue or a red dress, and then you look at these bishops who work every day putting their lives on the line for Jesus Christ. You look at the world and think, people are starving and all this is going on and my problems are minuscule compared to what they're dealing with. It brings every-thing into focus being here with all these bishops. Some of them, when they go home, may be facing persecution, possible imprisonment, and even death. You look at that and you say, 'my life is easy.' I have Jesus Christ in my life and I don't have to pay a terrible penalty for that bless-ing. Some of these bishops do. It makes it all seem really—awesome!"

Between Libby's baptism and her arrival at Canterbury she took ownership of her faith. She recalls the turbulence of adolescence and especially remembers the trauma of being someone important in the eighth grade to being a nobody at the bottom of the heap in senior high school. She mourns the loss of childhood friends who got caught up in the culture of drugs and sex. What literally saved her from going that route was her experience at age 15 in the ninth grade on a "Happening" weekend.

Happening is a weekend retreat for adolescents, which provides them with a strong presentation of God's love for them and a warm experience of Christian community. It is a junior edition of the Cursillo Weekend that has been a source of renewal in the Roman Catholic, Episcopal, Lutheran, Methodist, and Presbyterian churches.

Libby reports that she knew that her parents, "had a Lord and that they knew who he was."

"Christ became my Christ on that weekend," Libby states. She had been moved by the presentations, by the joy and caring and love that was in the community, and by the letters of love and encouragement she received that weekend from her parents, her older sister, her friends, and the leaders of the Happening. At the closing service, with the chapel illuminated only by candle light, the group was singing a song about, the presence of Christ, "Have you ever stood in the family, with the Lord there in your midst, Seen the face of Christ on your neighbor? Then I say you've seen Jesus my Lord."* She looked across the room and everyone was singing and crying. It was then that she decided, "This is the real thing." The cross was glowing in the candlelight. "It was just at that moment that I said, 'He's here!'"

But it wasn't just one moment for Libby. It was knowing that she was part of a community which shared in this experience. "We had a lot in common." she said. Libby and the others at the weekend were "grasping him" for themselves. "You bring Christ into your heart," she concluded. "It was not just a moment, it was like I was pulling him in. Awesome!"

What difference has that experience made in Libby's life? "It's like having someone in your corner helping you out," she declares with echoes of joy in her voice.

She also reports that she sees things differently, "now that I know Christ." She wonders how anyone can see a bird or look at a sunset or any other part of God's creation and attribute it to chance. "I've been given a different view of the world."

And that view includes serving other people. She wants to "give something back." On entering the University of North Carolina in the fall of 1998, she planed to major in music, the performing arts, and biology. Her long-range goal is to follow in her father's foot steps and go to medical school.

Recalling the experience of her grandfather, "who was a good Southern Baptist, knew his Bible, and lived to be 85," she says she wants to be a doctor for older people.

"I just love older people. They are so cute," she says. "I love being here (at Lambeth) because I see all these old decrepit bishops."

Scripture

> The Lord is my shepherd; I shall not want.
> He maketh me to lie down in green pastures;
> He leadeth me beside the still waters.
> He restoreth my soul;
> He leadeth me in the paths of righteousness for his Name's sake.
> Yea, though I walk through the valley of the shadow of death,
> I will fear no evil; for thou art with me;
> Thy rod and thy staff they comfort me.
> Thou preparest a table before me in the presence of mine enemies;
> Thou anointest my head with oil; my cup runneth over.
> Surely, goodness and mercy shall follow me all the days of my life,
> And, I will dwell in the house of the Lord forever.

Psalm 23
King James version

Reflection

I didn't think that the bishops looked "decrepit." In fact I had just the opposite reaction. Actually, I thought that most of them looked rather young. I guess it's all a matter of perspective. At eighteen, everyone over forty looks old. And from the perspective of the sixties, anyone under fifty still has the energy and glow of youth!

How refreshing to meet someone like Libby, who had been touched by the stories of Christians living in the other two thirds of the world!

How moving to hear her grief over the members of her own generation whose lives had been wounded by the drug culture.

How grateful I am that the church was there for Libby and that there was a "Happening" weekend where she could "meet Jesus my Lord."

How grateful I am for great grandmother Tilly and all the other members of her family who encouraged her in learning the 23 rd. Psalm and "all other things a Christian ought to know and believe for their soul's health."

It is my hope that in hearing the stories of others in their faith journey that the reader will be able to connect with parts of their own stories. Hearing Libby tell of her first exposure to "The Lord is my shepherd," activated the early childhood section of my memory bank. For me it was a thunderstorm in the middle of a summer night. I was terrified and crawled into my parents' bed.

What do you remember?

Hymn

Onward Christian Soldiers,
Marching as to war,
With the cross of Jesus
Going on before!
Christ, the royal master,
Leads against the foe;

Forward into battle,
See, his banners go.

REFRAIN

Onward Christian Soldiers,
Marching as to war,
With the cross of Jesus
Going on before!

At the sign of triumph
Satan's host doth flee;
On, then, Christian soldiers,
On to victory!
Hell's foundations quiver
At the shout of praise;
Brothers lift your voices,
Loud your anthems raise.

REFRAIN

Like a mighty army
Moves the church of God;
Brothers, we are treading
Where the saints have trod;
We are not divided,
All one body we,
One in hope and doctrine,
One in charity.

REFRAIN

Crowns and thrones may perish,
Kingdoms rise and wane,
But the Church of Jesus
Constant will remain;
Gates of hell may never
'Gainst the Church prevail;
We have Christ's own promise,
And that cannot fail.

REFRAIN

Onward, then, ye people,
Join our happy throng;
Blend with ours your voices
In the triumph song:
Glory, laud and honor,
Unto Christ the King;
This through countless ages
Men and angels sing.

REFRAIN

Sabine Baring-Gould
1982 Episcopal Hymnal, #562

* *Jesus My Lord* by John Fisher, 1970 Songs and Creations, Inc.

Chapter Fifteen

Dr. Livingstone, I presume?

Bernard Bagaba

We used to play "Stanley and Livingstone" in the marsh behind the public school. It was a form of hide and seek and was based on the movie of the same name. Everybody went to the movies on Saturday morning. There was a main feature (often a double feature), cartoons, and then an installment of a Tom Mix or Flash Gordon serial. And it was all for the price of 25 cents! The film "Stanley and Livingstone" was a big hit and left a lasting impression on our gang of fourth graders. It was about a reporter from the New York Herald, Henry Morton Stanley, who went into darkest Africa searching for the missionary doctor, David Livingstone, who had not been heard from for a long time.

The game we played in the marsh, they call them wetlands now, was a form of hide and seek. The designated "Dr. Livingstone" would have thirty seconds in which to hide in the tall grass before the rest of us would begin "to explore." Instead of the familiar catch line, "You're it," we would tag our victim with the famous line, delivered by Spencer Tracy in the movie, "Dr. Livingstone, I presume." As I recall, the game went on for about six weeks, until an even more compelling Tarzan movie captured our imaginations. But before we left "Stanley and Livingstone" our Sunday school class picked up on the theme and we took up a special offering for the "missionaries in darkest Africa." What we didn't know, and probably had no way of knowing, was that the missionary work of the late nineteenth century had truly taken root in many parts of Africa.

About the time I was hiding in the bulrushes, a significant religious renewal movement was sweeping through the Christian communities of East Africa. Called the East African Revival, its basic premise was to teach people to "walk in the light." Among those who responded to the crusade were the parents of Bernard Begaba. They lived on a farm in a remote upcountry area of Uganda. They had married in their village's Anglican church. They could neither read nor write. They took their eight children to be baptized and then to church and to Sunday school each week. They told them bible stories at bedtime, helped them with their prayers, and sang them to sleep with simple Christian songs. Bernard remembers his father saying grace in his native Bantu, "Lord be with us here as we share this meal. We thank you for giving us this meal. In Jesus Christ our Lord we pray. Amen." The meal of beans, potatoes, peanuts, millet, sorghum, peas, cabbage, and coffee came from their own garden. And then there was livestock: chickens, goats, and sheep.

The Begaba family bartered their surplus and managed to keep a well-stocked larder. But it took the efforts of the entire family for them to live slightly above the subsistence level. Bernard was assigned the job of minding the sheep and goats. Despite the biblical precedent for a young boy having such a job, he does not remember being a particularly good or happy shepherd. He recalls musing, "I am a slave to these animals. If we could kill them and eat them, I could go to school." He was eleven when a younger brother came along to take his place and Bernard entered the village school where he learned to read and write. At about that same time two things happened. He was confirmed in the local church with other boys and girls his age. It was part of growing up, but it didn't have any great impact on his life. The second event had to do with the terrorist tactics of Uganda's ruthless leader Idi Amin—and left a lasting impression.

Bernard remembers soldiers coming into his village looking for members of rival leader Obote's tribe. Those were bad times economically and there were a lot of shortages. You couldn't get any salt or sugar and his father couldn't sell his coffee. People who claimed to represent the government would come by and take the coffee beans and leave a receipt for them, but the receipts weren't any good. Some of the local farmers would take their coffee over the border into the Republic of Congo, but that was considered smuggling and you could be put in jail or shot for it if you were caught. Idi Amin's days in power were bad times for Bernard and his family.

"Then," Bernard remembers, "we heard on the radio that Archbishop Janani Luwum had been killed in an automobile accident, along with two cabinet ministers." Bernard later learned that the Primate of Uganda had actually been murdered and that Bishop Festo Kivengere, Bernard's own bishop, was next on the government's "hit list." It was not an easy time to be a Christian, an Anglican, or just an ordinary person in Uganda.

Bernard was a good student and when he completed the fifth grade in the village school, his father's farm income had improved enough for him to send Bernard to an Anglican boarding school to complete his secondary education. When he graduated, he remained at the school as a teacher.

At age 28, while teaching a class, Bernard heard a song that changed his life. While school was in session, there was a revival going on in the church next door. Bernard heard the congregation singing:

> *My son, you see all of the things I have done for you.*
> *I died for you on the cross.*
> *I shed my blood for your sake.*
> *Now let me ask you this, my child,*
> *Do you love me?*
> *A woman can forget her child,*
> *But let me tell you,*
> *I am not like that.*

The song was in Bernard's own language and he had heard it many times before. But he had never really thought about the question, "Do you love me?"

"There I was in the classroom teaching the children. I heard the people singing and the words had fresh meaning for me, as if I had never heard them before. The song spoke to me. I gave the children an assignment and I told them that when they finished it they could either go to the mission next door in the church or go home, if they preferred. I excused myself and went to the mission."

Bernard picked a seat in the back row. "I didn't want to sit in the middle because I didn't want to be that much involved in the mission. Then they sang the song again with that ringing question, 'Do you love me?'" He was very uncomfortable and said to himself, "What do I do? What do I do?"

Then the music stopped and everyone went home for lunch.

Bernard covered the four-mile trail to his home village in record time. His wife had placed his lunch on the table, but he could not eat it. He went to his bed and lay down. In two minutes, he was back on his feet, passed his lunch right by, and ran back to the church.

"This time I went somewhere in the middle of the church—not at the back this time. They started preaching again. People were standing up and giving their testimonies; telling everybody what they had done wrong and how they had been forgiven. They confessed all kinds of things I hadn't done: adultery, stealing, brutality. But there were lots of other things mentioned that I had done-or left undone that I should have done. Then they started singing that song again."

About the third time around with singing, "Do you love me?" the leader asked, "Who wants to commit his life to the Lord?" Bernard raised his hand.

When the leader saw Bernard's hand in the air, he smiled and said, "OK, now stand up!" Bernard held onto his seat.

A fellow teacher sitting next to Bernard leaned over and whispered, "You put your hand up, you started to stand up, and now you're sitting down. Why don't you make up your mind?"

Bernard recalls, "I knew it was my friend speaking, but it was as though the Lord was speaking to me through him."

Bernard stood up and his friend laughed and said, "For what are you standing?" Bernard almost sat down again. It was now or never. Trembling, he moved toward the altar.

"I declared myself as a person who had accepted Jesus Christ. From that day, in fact, I have felt a great difference. The Lord has done a lot in my life; he has taken me from strength to strength, from glory to glory. I was only a grade school teacher and now the Lord has taken me through all stages of education and now I am a priest of the Church of Uganda!"

Bernard and his wife Maude have six children, four of their own and two they have adopted. The adopted children are a niece and nephew whose parents died of AIDS. It is estimated that more than 10% of the people of Uganda are HIV positive.

I met Bernard on the campus of the University of Kent, Canterbury. He was in England completing work on an Master's degree and had volunteered to work as a steward at the Lambeth Conference. Before coming to the UK, he had served as a hospital chaplain, pastor, and priest. What would he do when he returned to his homeland? He smiled, "I don't know what I will be doing. I am anxious to see what work the Lord has for me to do." And then he added, "I have been blessed with an Abraham kind of faith. The eye of faith tells me that God is in control. I follow him, I accept him as my personal savior, and I trust him in all that I do."

Scripture

Have faith in God. Truly, I tell you, if you say to this mountain, 'be taken up and thrown into the sea,' and if you do not doubt in your heart, but believe that what you say will come to pass, it will be done for you. So I tell you, whatever you ask for in prayer, believe that you have received it, and it will be yours.

Mark 11:22-24
NRSV

Reflection

Like many other people, Bernard first chose John 3:16 when I asked him for his favorite line of scripture: "For God so loved the world that he gave his only son so that everyone who believes in him may not perish, but have eternal life." This passage seems to find an open window into people's lives. Having seen it so many times spray painted on walls and displayed at ball games, I confess that I have become somewhat desensitized to its power to penetrate the human heart. Like the hymn, "Amazing Grace," it carries the good news of the Gospel in a form that can be readily received. Sometimes, I suspect that those of us who are clergy miss the boat by not listening to what people are saying and not paying attention to what they respond to—to what attracts them simply and powerfully.

Bernard's story is typical of many that I heard, especially from Africa. He grew up in a Christian home and heard the " Christian story" many times: in scripture, in prayer, in song, and in the liturgy of the church. He received the sacrament of Baptism at birth and was confirmed at the age of puberty. He led a decent life, but something was missing until he made a personal commitment to the Lord. Then new things began to happen and, to use C. S. Lewis' phrase, he was "surprised by joy" and driven into the Lord's service.

This might be a good time to reflect on your own spiritual journey. Have you heard enough of the Gospel to make you uncomfortable but not joyful? Is it a control issue with you? Do all of us want to be "in charge" of our own lives or are we willing to make a leap of faith and turn it over to God? That's something to think about and to pray about.

Hymn

I praise you Jesus Christ,
           Son of God,
Who shed his blood for me,
           And the blood that washes the sinner,
And therefore I thank you,
           My saviour.

Ugandan Folk Hymn.

Chapter Sixteen

Cool!

Paul Gregory McKenzie

"Cool," is the word that comes to mind when I recall my visit with Paul Gregory McKenzie from Auckland, New Zealand. When I first met him on the Kent University campus he reminded me of a surfer in search of a big wave. He was tall and slender, his long hair was sun streaked, he had a smile on his face and he...well, he just looked cool.

At age 24, with a college degree, being at Canterbury was for Paul, "a matter of timing." He has broken up with his girl friend and he had been working as a cleaner at the Cathedral in Auckland. After a year he decided to leave the job. He had wanted to work with youth ministry as well as a mop and a broom, but couldn't find any interest in joining in such a ministry and so it was time to move on. "They were very good to me as a cleaner, but bad to me as a Christian who wanted to be involved in youth ministry."

Paul heard about the need for volunteers at the Lambeth Conference and he thought that would be "cool" and so there he was.

When I asked him who his heroes might be, he immediately named his biblical namesake, St. Paul. Why Paul? "I could be seduced by travel," stated Paul McKenzie, "and St. Paul was a traveler. He was a traveler with a purpose, unlike all of my counterparts tripping, junketing around the world spending money on themselves. We all think that's a cool thing to do. But what Paul was doing was *really* a cool thing. He was absolutely solid in his sacrifice to Christ, commitment, and complete willingness to give his life to and for the Gospel, doing it all not taking any half measures."

131

He said that he had always been a Christian, that "he had always known the love of God in his life." He had been baptized as an infant and confirmed when he was fifteen. After saying that he didn't have a point where he could say, "that's where I became a Christian." He noted that he was too young when he was confirmed and that confirmation was mainly "a cultural thing," and that the "reconfirmation" of his being a Christian had happened many times over.

Paul's father was a teacher and his mother a housewife and mother to Paul and his brother and sister. Paul was the middle child. The McKenzie family was comfortably middle-class in Parnell, New Zealand. They attended an Anglican church with a charismatic emphasis. Young Paul liked the worship there, worship that, in Paul's words, "expresses a solid faith, is focused on Jesus and is joyful." The solid Christian commitment of his parents, his parish church and their youth group, saved him from the "Cannabis Culture" and "rough teens" in New Zealand.

Under the heading or "reconfirmation," he points to a youth weekend in the charismatic tradition when he was 20 years old. He felt the calling of God in his life. He speaks of "grieving in the Spirit; praying, but not using words. There's almost nothing on your mind. You don't try to say things, you let the Holy Spirit work on your spirit at the deepest level. I had things to sort out. Things to grieve for. I just cried and I wasn't even able to express why I was crying. You're crying in the spirit because there are things that have gone wrong in your life-so you cry."

And then there are the cries of joy, not grief. "Like you can be joyous, like sometimes you can cry out of joy for the love of God." He smiled and laughed. His laughter was genuine and infectious. "You're astonished and astounded by the love of Christ in your life," he continued. "You're happy, pure happiness just welling up from within your heart and your soul." He laughed "Are you a married man? Are you in love with your wife?" he asked me.

"Both," I answered.

"It's like that first initial falling in love feeling," he went on. "You're on top of the world, on a deeper level. It's just being happy at a divine level. Sometimes being a Christian is a struggle and sometimes it's just—Wow!"

"What about the struggle?" I asked.

He spoke of "spiritual warfare" and he spoke of there being a "dark side." You feel the Love of God in your life, but you also feel the calling of many other lusts. Money, women, jobs, cars—all pull in the opposite direction. I felt that God was moving in my life in a powerful way through his Holy Spirit. But I also came into a lot of temptation, especially with women." He laughed again and then concluded, "You can be going somewhere with God and then crash."

He spoke of his summer in England as "a bridge" He had been offered a three month internship in a charismatic parish when he got back to New Zealand, but he said that he was really looking for some sort of "unpaid ministry working with people." He talked about "serving people and standing alongside the marginalized." Before coming to England he had been supporting a friend in her grief over her fiancee, a mountain climber, who had been lost in an avalanche. He had also spent time at a Franciscan mission in Parnell, New Zealand, where the brothers feed the homeless from their verandah. "I got to know a few of the street people and something about their culture." He remembered a fairly young alcoholic, "who had once been a world champion athlete," He said, with a sigh, that they had talked for over an hour but a week later the athlete had no memory of ever having met him. Paul made reference several times to evangelism, but then added that he didn't know how to do evangelism, "certainly not in the traditional sense of the term. I don't think God is calling me to be a preacher."

The experience of Lambeth was a "bridge" for him personally, but did nothing to change his impression of the institutional church. He wondered about the expense of bringing 750 bishops together from all over the world, not to mention support staff like himself. As for the deliberations on the subject of sexuality, he found himself in the middle. "I can't support the gay bashers, nor the priests who want to live in a homosexual relationship." He said, "I believe that marriage is the holy order where a sexual relationship is appropriate; where it is blessed by God and where there can be a healthy relationship." But then he added that what he had kept looking for in the sexuality debates, and did not find was "a call to holiness."

Paul and I shook hands and wished each other well. As he strolled off to attend to his assigned duties, I thought again of the surfer in search of the big one.

Scripture

Blessed are the poor in spirit, for theirs is the Kingdom of Heaven..
Blessed are those who mourn, for they will be comforted.
Blessed are the meek, for they will inherit the earth.
Blessed are those who hunger and thirst for righteousness, for they will be filled.
Blessed are the merciful, for they will receive mercy.
Blessed are the pure in heart, for they will see God.
Blessed are the peacemakers, for they will be called children of God.
Blessed are those who are persecuted for righteousness sake, for theirs is the kingdom of heaven.

Blessed are you when people revile you and persecute you and utter all kinds of evil against you falsely on my account. Rejoice and be glad for your reward is in heaven, for in the same way they persecuted the prophets who were before you.

Matthew 5:1-11
NRSV

Reflection

Paul McKenzie was definitely a work in progress. He was bright, articulate, and attractive. He loves the Lord and has a genuine love for people and a desire to help. While I could think of many scripture passages as we talked, I could not help thinking how much the concerns of this searching, contemporary young man resonated with the concerns of the ancient Beatitudes

Like many of his generation he is not so much turned off by the institutional church, but indifferent to it. I personally found his identification of St. Paul as a traveler to be a fresh insight. A cruise ship chaplain once told me that Europeans and North Americans tend to leave their religion at home, while the seafaring Philippinos who crew many of the ships take their religion with them. No wonder St. Paul the traveler had so much to say about the Holy Spirit! Reflecting on my own ministry as a parish priest, I grieve over those good and decent people who participated in and contributed to the life of a church in their home town only to become spiritual orphans when they moved on. Saul of Tarsus, the Pharisee, knew with certainty that the YHWH of the Torah dwelt in the Holy of Holies in Jerusalem, but a renewed, expanded, completed and converted Paul, the Apostle, would say to the Athenians assembled on Mars Hill, "The God who made the world and everything in it , he who made heaven and earth, does not live in shrines made of human hands......he is not far from each one of us. For, 'In him we live and move and have our being.'"(Acts 17:24-28.)

Hymn

Thine be the glory, risen, conquering Son,
endless is the victory thou o'er death hast won;
angels in bright raiment rolled the stone away,
kept the folded grave-clothes where the body lay.

REFRAIN
  Thine be the glory,risen, conquering Son,
  endless is the victory thou o're death hast won.

Lo, Jesus meets us, risen from the tomb;
lovingly he greets us, scatters fear and gloom;
let the church with gladness hymns of triumph sing,
for her Lord now liveth, death hath lost its sting:

REFRAIN

No more we doubt thee, glorious Prince of Life;
life is nought without thee: aid us in our strife;
make us more than conquerors through thy deathless love;
bring us safe through Jordan to thy home above:

REFRAIN

E.L. Budry (1854-1932)
tr. R.B. Hoyle (1875-1939)
Hymns Ancient and Modern, #428

Chapter Seventeen

Look Under "G" For God

Susan Howatch

It had all of the trappings of a revival meeting, including a tent full of people who were there for religious purposes. As it turned out, conversion was one of the topics of conversation. But it wasn't a religious revival; at least not in the classical sense.

The location of the gathering was in the spouses tent on the campus of the University of Kent, Canterbury, England at the 1998 Lambeth Conference. Most of the more than 700 bishops came with their spouses. Earlier Lambeths had gatherings for bishops' wives. But with eleven women bishops, the term "spouse" was needed. Five male spouses attended Lambeth and participated in the activities at the Spouses Tent, while their episcopal wives were otherwise occupied.

Eileen Carey, spouse of the Archbishop of Canterbury, welcomed the overflow crowd. They had gathered under the canvas to hear the popular British author, Susan Howatch. Her claim to fame, as far as the prelates were concerned, came from five romantic novels that involved Church of England clergy in and about a fictitious cathedral city known as Starbridge. Often referred to as the Anthony Trollope of the 20th century, Howatch wrote of vulnerable human beings who always run the danger of being "fatally cut off from the God they're trying to serve." She brought the house down when she mentioned a clergyman in her new book, *The Wonder Worker*, whose most redeeming feature was "that he had no desire to be a bishop." And, again, when she mentioned the plight of the lonely clergy wife whose husband is, "out being wonderful somewhere else." In the process of her presentation, her own Christian commitment and theological convictions emerged. "Real Christianity is a way of life," she said, "a way of making sense of things, which leads to a lifestyle and a mind-set that is distinctly at odds with so many of the lifestyles and mind-sets currently in fashion."

She brought her audience to their feet when she compared her own efforts as a writer with her understanding of redemption. When an author finally holds a printed novel in her/his hands:

It's then that a strange thing happens. You know that every word you've written has been redeemed. It's as if the scrunched-up sheets of paper and all the poor little crossed out words rise up out of the waste paper basket, each one of them shining and precious and vibrant with meaning. And this transformation—this resurrection—is so because I could never have reached the final draft without all those wrong turnings and discarded efforts, without all those failures and all those mistakes, and all that backbreaking mess. In the end, I promise you, nothing is wasted and everything is resurrected and redeemed. I know that every little word has its purpose, even the briefest and most short lived. And every little word is honored and cherished by me, the author, as I hold the printed work in my hands. The printed book is the memorial, not only of all the words between the covers, of the novel, but of all the words which passed through my mind during that chaotic, painful, but infinitely worthwhile creative process.

Acquiring the faith which she so eloquently expressed and which the prelates applauded was not something Susan had come by easily. What follows is in part what she said to the bishops and their spouses at

Canterbury, and it is, in part, from a conversation I had with Susan Howatch at 6 Amen Court in London, following the Conference. I thought it was very gracious of Ms. Howatch to walk from her apartment in the Barbican to Amen Court near St. Paul's. But, she assured me that graciousness had nothing to do with it. "I wasn't about to let a strange man into my flat!"

Susan's Church of England baptism, was in no way reinforced by her family attending church or taking her to Sunday school. Her only exposure to the Gospel was the religious instruction she received in school. She knew the stories, but had no idea how they applied to her own life. By the time she was in her thirties, God was, in her own words, "similar to Mount Everest-very impressive, but a long way away, and of no possible relevance to my life."

At that time, she returned to England with her daughter after a failed marriage to an American. Nevertheless, her career as an international best-selling author of romantic novels had, from a financial point of view, been a success for twelve years. Then one morning she woke up and realized that everything that she had thought was important was not important and, "everything I had thought was irrelevant was actually very relevant indeed. So, it was like a 360 degree turn," she recalled. She was living, at the time, in Salisbury, in the Cathedral Close. Her personal crisis of meaning had been sparked by a conversation with her English publisher, who reacted to delays in completing her latest novel by saying, "Oh, what am I going to tell the accountants at the board meeting?" She became disillusioned with all she had worked to achieve professionally, "if all my writing had to do was keeping the publishers in the black, then what was life all about?" She saw herself as a failure, as a wife and mother, but as an ambitious writer, she considered herself a great success. Now, even that was in question. She just wasn't satisfied and she thought, "There must be another option." She remembered, from the religious instruction she received in school, the concept that, "if you serve God instead of yourself, that is the road to a better sort of

life. Why not give it a try? The only trouble was not coming from a religious family. I knew nothing about God. So I went to the public library
and looked under 'G' for God." Actually, she confesses to embellishing
the story a bit. She started with "Religious Studies," got to Christianity
and "went through the library like a vacuum cleaner." Of particular help
was an entry on "The Second Journey" in the *Dictionary of Christian
Spirituality*. "I realized that this was what I was going through. You get
to the crossroads and you can either go on," she reflects, "or you can
turn aside and do something new." Was she simply describing a mid-life
crisis under a religious title? An emphatic "no" was her response. Then
she went on to explain that a mid-life crisis has to do with trying to hold
onto, or recapture, one's youth. "When you take up with a 20 year old
blonde or a 25 year old boy toy, buy a sports car, cling to a lost youth
and you can't move on, you've got into a rut. While in the 'Second
Journey,' you want to let go of that. You want to move on; you've done
that; you let go of your youth; you want to move on; but you don't know
where you want to go. You want to embrace middle age and all of its
creative possibilities."

The article was reassuring and a turning point for Susan. "That entry
described exactly what I'd been going through—and I can't tell you
what a relief it was to discover that I wasn't going mad, but was instead
experiencing a classic form of a well known and not uncommon spiritual syndrome. For a long time, for many months, I wasn't sure what I
was going to do. I was waiting for God to give me an answer," she
remembers.

At first she thought she ought to enroll in a graduate program in theology. But that wasn't the way. Then she recalls, "a creative burst" in
which she went on as a writer, but writing something quite different.
Living in the Close of Salisbury Cathedral, she invented a cathedral city,
Starbridge. It was very different from anything she had written before,
"but my attitude was different," she explains. In the past she would have
begun with the attitude that, "I hope this makes the best seller list and I

hope I make a nice million bucks." Instead, she thought, "I'm going to offer it to God." And even if it only sells a dozen copies, at least God could use them in that way. "All I've got to do," she told herself, "is to write the book as best I can and then leave it to God." When she finished what was to be *Glittering Images*, she set it aside, quite unsure of whether anyone would like it or any publisher would print it. She was well into her second Starbridge volume, *Glamorous Powers*, when she had the courage to share her new work with both her British and American agents. Much to her delight they both, and quite independently, responded in the affirmative. "They were both very keen that I should publish them. That was the green light, the answer I was looking for that I should go ahead." At the time she was leading the life of a, "recluse. I really didn't really see anyone; all I did was read and study and write."

One of her few human contacts was an old retired priest, the Vicar of the Close, who did the pastoral work for the cathedral. "At one stage, I was in such despair that he did the laying on of hands." It was her first experience of the ministry of healing, but at the time it was not appreciated. "It was absolutely frightful," she said. "I just couldn't bear it. It was absolutely vile. I was so upset."

In *Scandalous Risks*, she describes a similar incident in the life of her heroine, Venetia.

> *Father Darrow, quite without warning, laid his hands on my head and pressed down so strongly that I nearly collapsed. My mind went blank. I felt as if I had been given an electric shock ....I ducked away from his hands, grabbed the rim of the table and hauled myself to my feet.*

Like the character in her fourth book, Susan Howatch was angry and confused. She got in her car and drove up to the top of Old Sarum Hill, where the archeological outline of the first cathedral can still be seen.

She just sat there in turmoil, fuming, "That was absolutely dreadful. I couldn't bear it. Of course I was so angry and I let it all out. It was so ridiculous."

Part of her anger was directed at herself, "What was all that about? All that rubbish. Why couldn't I just pull myself up by my bootstraps and move on? It was the old Pelagian heresy." But it was a healing experience and the next morning she felt calm. In her latest work, *The Wonder Worker,* set in one of London's old City churches, she deals with the subject of spiritual healing, which had it's beginning in her own healing in Salisbury. Years later, she met the old Vicar of the Close, hugged him, and kissed him on both cheeks.

While the Sarum experience was a "letting go of guilt and anger," she believes that, "It was an important experience, but it was all part of a continuing unfolding. "I came to Christianity by the intellect, by reading, which is supposed to be impossible, but all I can say is that's the way it happened, by the intellect, by reading." But having said that she adds, "Before I started reading, it was God who reached out to me. When I felt such a failure, I felt that I was being stripped of everything that was important to me. I was sitting in the Close at the time and the Cathedral became very much a living presence. I could feel it out there. What it was representing was God, a sign pointing beyond itself to the reality which was still hidden from my conscious mind."

Susan moved from Salisbury to London in 1986, where she settled into a flat near Westminster Abbey. She later moved to the Barbican, which is within walking distance of St. Paul's Cathedral. In spite of her affinity for large historic churches, worship is not something that came easily or followed immediately upon her conversion. In Salisbury she took long walks around the Cathedral, but seldom attended services. "I was on the outside, looking in." At Westminster, she entered the Abbey, but would, "hide behind a pillar." At St. Paul's she often attends evensong, which she describes as her favorite service. "Worship was the very last thing I came to. I found it very difficult," she states. "The old Vicar of the Salisbury Close once told her that worship had to be worked at. As soon as I realized that worship had nothing to do with entertainment, I was fine. When I saw it as a discipline and a framework, I began to make progress."

What is the discipline of worship? "Just turning up and being there," she states. "If you turn up and offer yourself to God, then something will happen." She likens the discipline of worship to the advice she gives to aspiring writers (including this one). "Just go to your typewriter every day and just sit there for four hours and eventually something will happen. You'll be so damn bored, that eventually something will happen. The same is true about prayer. Everything that is said about prayer, I can parallel with the writing process, the creative effort." She added, "The actual business of liturgy, I find almost impossible to understand. But I do show up."

Susan began writing novels in which clergy play a leading role, "Because one of the most impressive things about Christianity was the fact that many dynamic and brilliant people had found it credible, with the result that many of those people wound up as clerics. I, therefore, had no hesitation in deciding that my clergymen were going to be clever, personable and interesting."

She also has no hesitation of dealing with clergy weakness, frailty, and vulnerability. Discovering clerical dysfunction has in no way diminished her own faith. She says that "People are my business. I couldn't write about clergy without thinking of them as people. If you understand people, you will forgive them. My job is to get to know them so well as to empathize and sympathize with them. When I started writing, I didn't know anything about clergy breakdown, but I thought it must happen because they are human. I never saw them as idealized people. I didn't come from a church background." She recoils at the suggestion that she writes about "vicars and knickers." "Some people get so hung up on the sins," she observes, "that they miss the major themes of repentance, forgiveness, and redemption."

She makes no apology for having traveled the difficult intellectual route to faith. Not surprisingly, Augustine of Hippo is one of her heroes. "He had a brilliant intellect and was a very sexy man, who chose Christianity because nothing satisfied him intellectually. He had tried other things which didn't get him anywhere. Christianity packs a very powerful intellectual clout. When you think of all those world religions, with the exception of Islam, developing in the first thousand years BC, Christianity is by far the most sophisticated. Christianity has been going for 2,000 years and the cracks have been beaten out of it. So you're dealing with something that the best minds in the Western Europe have been concentrating on for 2,000 years. And that means a good deal. I had to have something that was intellectually respectable. "

Scripture

All things work together for those who love God; for them who are called according to his purpose.

Romans 8:28

Reflection

Susan stumbled on the above passage from Romans at a time when she was going through a difficult time and was quite depressed. She heard a sermon in Guildford Cathedral in which the preacher began by quoting the passage and the comment, "tell that to the person who's dying of cancer." She recalled that was exactly how she felt. It was followed by a sermon on redemption, which has become one of the recurring themes in her books.

I had never heard of "the second journey" until my conversation with Ms. Howatch and I have shared it with many parishioners, especially those of middle years and beyond. It has been received with a sigh of relief and with the joy of anticipation that God wasn't finished with them yet and that maybe, as in the miracle of Cana, (John 2:1-12) he had saved the best to last. When I returned to Miami, I shared that concept with an adult Bible class. A week later I received a note from a lady whose mother had gone to her priest to "arrange her own funeral." She brought along her favorite hymns and scripture passages and then ended with the request that she be buried with a fork in her right hand. "When I was a little girl," she explained, "we always knew that mother had baked a pie or a cake, when we started to clear the table after the main course. 'Save your fork,' always alerted us that there was a wonderful surprise and a delicious treat in store."

Susan told me that while, "God reached out to me," she also had to deal with a great many intellectual issues. I saw a poster once that declared, "Jesus died to wipe out our sins, not our minds." It implied that while becoming a Christian is a supernatural event, that it is not irrational and that in answering the call of Christ we are not being asked to check our minds at the church door and that being a Christian is an intellectually respectable venture. (See Augustine, chapter 19 and C. S. Lewis, chapter 23.) What are the questions you have that need to be explored? What are the questions that keep you from fully owning the promises of your baptism?

I also find it most interesting that God did not send Susan off to a theological seminary, but put her right back at the word processor to write novels in which God's love, forgiveness and redemption were key issues. I remember Eugenia Price, the American novelist, telling me that she was afraid that if she became a Christian she would have to "stand on a street corner, with my slip showing, handing out religious tracts." Was it not Thomas Aquinas who said, "Grace does not destroy nature, it perfects it."

As we have already noted, Susan grew up with out any formal Sunday school or church experience. The hymn, which she selected, was learned at school assembly in England. It had little, if any, meaning at the time she first heard it, but it stayed with her, somewhere deep down in her memory bank, until she went looking for God in the library. What does this say about what we learn as children? What does this say about what we teach our own children?

Hymn

Through all the changing scenes of life,
In trouble and in joy,
The praises of my God shall still
My heart and tongue employ.

O magnify the Lord with me,
with me exalt his name;
when in distress to him I called,
he to my rescue came.

The hosts of God encamp around
the dwellings of the just ;
deliverance he affords to all
who on his succor trust.

O make but trial of his love:
experience will decide
how blest are they, and only they,
who in his truth confide.

Fear him ye saints, and you will then
have nothing else to fear;
make you his service your delight,
…your wants shall be his care .

To Father, Son, and Holy Ghost,
the God who we adore,
be glory, as it was, is now,
and shall be evermore.

Tate and Brady, 1696
based on Psalm 34
Hymns, Ancient and Modern, #209

Chapter Eighteen

Tolle Lege, Tolle Lege

Augustine of Hippo

When Martin Luther and then John Wesley decided that we are saved by grace and not good works, they were building on a foundation already put down by St. Augustine. And we continue to build on it. When a Christian social activist calls the church to work for justice, when a pastor counsels a parishioner, whose world is falling apart, that in spite of evidence to the contrary, God is in charge, they are building on Augustine's foundation. When the Dean of Virginia Theological Seminary advised a future bishop that her baptism was valid or, for that matter, when a night club singer chants, "Che sera, sera!" they are all building on the thoughts of Augustine, the late fourth and early fifth century Bishop of Hippo in North Africa. No other theologian, with the possible exception of Thomas Aquinas, has had a greater impact on western civilization or on the way that Christians, Protestant and Catholic alike, sort out their world. Augustine, following in the tradition of St. Paul, wrote eloquently not only about his spiritual journey in his *Confessions* and other writings, but expounded on many issues central to Christianity: Original Sin, the Sovereignty of God, God's Grace, Predestination and Free Will. While my forebears, known as the barbarians, were sacking Rome, Augustine wrote of a world of justice and peace in *The City of God*.

There are three quotations that seem to capture the spiritual struggle that led to the Conversion of Augustine:

*You awake us to delight in your praise; for you made us
for yourself, and our hearts are restless until they find their
rest in you.*

Confessions I, 1

Give me chastity and continence, but not just now.

Confessions VII, 7

Take up and read.

Confessions VIII, 12

While the name *Monica* has become somewhat tarnished of late, there once was a St. Monica. She was a Christian married to a pagan Roman official in what is now Algeria in North Africa. There has been much speculation about their racial background and while there is very little evidence to back up any one theory, there is a strong tradition that Monica and her husband Patricus were Africans, and not just Romans stationed in a southern Mediterranean province. Their union produced Augustine on November 13, 354 AD. This was just 40 years after the ban against Christians was lifted by the Emperor Constantine. It was 29 years after the Council of Nicaea...

Augustine wasn't baptized as an infant. That's not the way things were done back then. Infant baptism was not the universal practice of the church until the fifth century. It was believed by some that baptism washed away all a person's sins prior to the sacrament, but that sins committed after baptism were a very serious matter and put one in danger of eternal damnation. This did not mean that Monica neglected her son's Christian development. She had a vision that her son had been created for a holy purpose, and that while Patricus might be Augustine's natural father, she was determined that God would be his spiritual father. She signed her son's forehead with the cross and sprinkled him with salt, a common practice at the time that usually began the catechetical process. But when as a child he was seized with excruciating stomach pains and was not expected to live, he cried out and pleaded for baptism. His mother was about to give into his request, when he recovered. The sacrament was deferred. Facing the turmoil of adolescence, Monica believed that the sins of youth were inevitable and that it was better that they be committed before baptism than after. "Let him be, let him do it, for he is not yet baptized," was a common saying of the day. Fornication was one thing, but doing it with someone's wife was the great no-no of adultery. Augustine, in reflecting back on his adolescent years, confessed that he liked doing what was unlawful, specifically, "because it was unlawful."

Monica and Patricus, like many modern parents, wanted the very best for their son and committed their meager income from the lower echelon of the Roman Civil Service toward his education. It began with the simple no nonsense approach of "learn your letters or we'll beat you." Underlying this methodology was the goal of subduing the will of the student. Augustine, with his creative and inquiring mind, chaffed under the system. He preferred sports and the adult entertainment of the arena and theater to his studies. First in Tagaste, then in Madura, and finally in Carthage, he was prepared for an academic career as a professor of rhetoric. In Carthage, when he was fifteen, he took a mistress, whose name he never mentioned. About this time his father was baptized and died shortly thereafter. By the time Augustine was 18 he himself became a father. His son was named Adeodatus, which is Latin for "gift of God." It was never suggested to him by his mother, his professors, or his classmates that he should wed the mother of his child.

While Christianity had the imperial blessing and a preferred position in the empire, it was by no means without competitors. Augustine's early Christian training rejected the fading image of the old Roman deities. His mother, of course, wanted him to be a Christian, but an early attempt to read the Bible had left him with more questions than it answered and then there were all the competing interpretations of the

Gospel message. They were known as heresies and included: Gnosticism, Arianism, Donatism, Nestorianism, and Pelagianism, as well as the Catholic faith of his mother. So, before he returned to Christianity he had to wrestle with all the options that the late Roman Empire had to offer. One of the young scholar's concerns was with the problem of evil. The teachings of the second century Mani of Persia had an attractive answer. In Manichaenism there was a synthesis or mixture of Gnostic Christianity, Persian Zoroastrianism, and Eastern mysticism, which dealt with the problem of good and evil by positing two creations, one by the good forces of light and the other by the evil powers of darkness. Mani had also drawn a caricature of Christ and Christianity in which he denounced and ridiculed the faith. For our young professor, this had great appeal. Manichaenism also had a moral code that more closely approximated young Augustine's testosterone level than did Christianity. For nine years, from age 19 to 28, Augustine was a Manichaean.

When Augustine, by age 28, had moved on to Rome, he had the opportunity to meet with Manichaean Bishop Faustus, whose reputation for eloquence and personal charm was well known. The encounter was a great disappointment. Faustus could not answer Augustine's questions, one of which had to do with the Christian scriptures. The Manichaeans contended that the New Testament had, wrote Augustine, "been tampered with by some unknown hand who wished to engraft the Jewish law on the Christian faith. But they themselves did not produce any uncorrupted copies." He noted sadly that he had learned a great lesson, "That the thing should not be considered true because it was well spoken, nor untrue because it came from a stammering tongue." The issue of style vs. substance is still with us. So is the debate regarding the origin and authenticity of the scriptures.

From Manichaeism he switched to Skepticism, which was not just a questioning attitude, but an established philosophical school of thought that simply advised suspended judgment. With a shrug of the shoulders, Skeptics declared that there are some things that can not be known. About this time Augustine had a life threatening illness, but unlike his reaction in childhood, he did not request baptism. Manichaeism, although it did not lend itself to logical scrutiny, had left a false image of Christianity in Augustine's mind. And the Manichaean conflict between matter and spirit made it difficult for Augustine to accept or even understand the basic Christian concept of the "word that became flesh and dwelt among us." (John 1:14) The idea of the incarnation, he thought, would be a defilement of the divine essence. This is a problem that, also, became a stumbling block for Muhammad. Skepticism, which concluded that there could be no conclusions, provided the future Bishop of Hippo with a resting place. This was followed by the stepping stone of Platonism, which cleared out the intellectual cobwebs of dualism and pointed to the intellectual respectability of Christianity. The Platonists, he said, "led to the belief in God and his word."

In his twenty-eighth year Augustine moved from Rome to Milan. This put him under the influence of the famous Ambrose, Bishop of Milan. He was known for his sermons and it was almost inevitable that Augustine, a professor of rhetoric, out of professional curiosity, would go to the cathedral to hear him preach. But, Ambrose, unlike Faustus, had substance as well as style. Week after week Augustine heard the bishop preach and little by little he came to the conclusion that Christianity could be intellectually respectable. Ambrose taught that there was one creation, not two, and that God had made everything, heaven and earth and all things visible and invisible. God's creation was not only good but "very good." Evil was the corruption or misuse of God's good creation. Satan was a fallen angel who had rebelled against his creator. From Ambrose's teaching Augustine would later refine his doctrine of the fall of man and original sin.

Ambrose was especially helpful in dealing with Augustine's concerns about scripture, especially the books of the Old Testament. Ambrose introduced him to the allegorical method of interpretation. Little by little he came to the conclusion that the scripture "could be defended without embarrassment." There had indeed been passages, "which interpreted literally" had killed him spiritually. The preaching of Ambrose was not only excellent rhetoric, but liberating intellectually and spiritually.

About the time Augustine arrived in Milan with his son and mistress, his mother, Monica, sensing her son's movement away from the Manichaeans and toward the Christians, also moved to Milan. She felt that her prayers for her son were being answered and she quickly dispatched Augustine's mistress back to Africa and began the search for a highly placed bride for her son. Augustine was rapidly becoming an academic star. There was even the possibility that he would be offered a post as an imperial governor. His career would be advanced if he had a wife "with some money so she would not be an added expense."

"My mistress," he wrote, "was torn from my side as a hindrance to my marriage. My heart which clung to her, was torn wounded and bleeding. She returned to Africa, vowing to you (God) never to know another man." He obviously loved the mother of his son. He complained to his diary, but he did nothing to stay his mother's managing role in his life. The chosen bride to be was underage and there was to be a two-year wait before the wedding.

With all of the intellectual problems concerning Christianity addressed, Augustine faced another contemporary problem. There was obviously a radical discontinuity between his life style and his belief. While he waited for his bride-to-be to mature, he acquired another mistress, whose name also remains a mystery. Thus we come to our second quote, " Give me chastity and continence, but not just now."

Then came the moment which would define the "before Christ" and the "years of our Lord" in his life. The issues had been clarified and the battle had been joined. He tried to resolve to put away his old ways and become a Christian, but then he would back away. One day he went off by himself and sat in a garden. He was in misery and he cried out, "How long? How long? Why is there not an end to my uncleanness this hour?" About this point he heard a child's voice singing, *tolle lege, tolle lege,* "Take up and read, take up and read." At first he thought the child was chanting the words to a children's song or game, like "The farmer in the dell" or "Ring around a rosie." The search engine in his brain came up with nothing. He then decided that it was "a command from God to pick up the Book and to read the first chapter I should find." This practice is often called biblical roulette and is frowned upon in academic circles. Augustine, however, did not know that. In fact he recalled that St. Antony had heard the words, "Go sell all that you have and give to the poor, and you shall have treasure in heaven and come follow me." (Matt. 19:21) So, Augustine turned to Paul's Letter to the Romans and read, "Not in reveling and drunkenness, not in debauchery and licentiousness, not in strife and envying, but put on the Lord Jesus Christ, and make no provision for the flesh to gratify its desires." (Romans 13:13)

Augustine read no further. He marked the passage with his finger and went home to share it with his best friend Alypius, who was also on the verge of becoming a Christian. Alyphius read the passage and then continued to discover the truth of, "Receive him that is weak in the faith." (Rom.14:1a) Augustine and his friend had crossed that invisible line: from uncertainty to faith; from despair to joy. The first thing they did was to tell Monica, who "leapt for joy":

For she perceived that you had given her more for me than she had praying for by her pitiful and most sorrowful groanings. For you converted me to yourself, so that I sought neither wife nor any other hope in the world-standing on that rule of faith on which you had showed me to her in a vision so many years before. And you turned her grief into a much more plentiful gladness than she had desired, and in much dearer and purer way than she used to crave when she asked for grandchildren of my body.

Augustine, along with his son, Adeodatus, and his friend Alypius were baptized by Bishop Ambrose at the Easter Vigil, Anno Domini 387. Monica who had prayed and worked to see that day, died shortly thereafter. Her purpose in life had been realized. In 391, at age 37, he was ordained a priest. Four years later he became Bishop of Hippo in North Africa, in which capacity he served for 35 years until his death on August 28, in 430.

Scripture

Besides this, you know what time it is, how it is now the moment for you to awake from sleep. For salvation is nearer to us now than when we became believers; the night is far gone, the day is near. Let us then lay aside the works of darkness and put on the armor of light; let us live honorably in the day, not in reveling and drunkenness, not in debauchery and licentiousness, not in quarreling and jealousy. Instead put on the Lord Jesus Christ, and make no provision for the flesh, to gratify its desires. Welcome those who are weak in the faith....

Romans 13: 11-14:1a
NRSV

Reflection

I would not even attempt to justify or explain any aspect of Augustine's relationship to, or treatment of, the women in his life. His mother is known as Saint Monica, and yet by contemporary standards she was on the surface, at least, a domineering and controlling mother. It's a shame we don't know the name of Augustine's mistress and

Adeodatus' mother, she certainly should be listed with the saints, and, in God's heart, probably is.

Susan Howatch said she liked Augustine because he had a first class mind and was also a sexy male. He certainly was that.

In the baptismal service in the American Book of Common Prayer, there is a prayer for the newly baptized that I often adapt for baccalaureate and graduations ceremonies. It reads in part, "Give *them* an inquiring and discerning heart, the courage to will and to persevere, a spirit to know and to love you, and the gift of joy and wonder in all your works. *Amen.*"

Augustine certainly had "an inquiring and discerning heart." God certainly used Augustine's inquiring nature to enrich the church and define the faith. As Ms. Howatch has indicated, coming to faith through the intellect is not an easy route, but it can be done. Simply put, Augustine was ready to hear the Gospel when he realized that Christianity provided a rational explanation of the world in which we live. His story also underlines the fact that conversion involves more than the mind.

We also see in Augustine's spiritual journey the importance of early childhood training. What he received from Monica as a little boy stayed with him even when he was off with the Manichaeans. Parents who say, "We're not going to impose our religion on our children, but let them decide for themselves when they grow up," should be charged with neglect and abuse. From what are they to choose? The drug culture? Satanism? Astrology? Self indulgence? Survival of the fittest?

Monica was also committed to pray for her son, which I assume included the petition, "Thy will be done." Monica's dream for Augustine was not totally spiritual. She wanted him to have the very best, which included: a rich wife, a big house, and a position of honor in the community. God's plan for her son was quite different. She prayed that he would come to faith and that prayer was answered. Maybe the Lord knew what he was doing when he called her home shortly after Augustine's baptism.

While it took Augustine a long time to appreciate the scriptures, once understood they became the cornerstone of his thinking and teaching. He took the scriptures very seriously, but was suspicious of a strictly literal reading of them. He saw the words as signs pointing beyond themselves to the reality of God's nature or God's will for God's people. In encouraging the study of the Bible, Augustine gave some helpful advice. Let me conclude this reflection with the following paraphrase of his thinking on the subject.

1. It isn't easy. You have to work at it. When you finally discover its meaning, you will have accomplished something and you will experience much joy. In other words, "No pain, no gain."

2. Read the canonical books of the Bible first, then go to the apocryphal writings.

3. Start with the clear parts, like the Gospels. Make sure you understand what they are saying. The Bible is a manual to encourage us to love God and our neighbor; to lead a life of charity. Look for clear rules of faith and/or rules of living.

4. Commit as much as you can to memory. A clear memory is more important than a good commentary

5. Go from the clear passages to the more obscure and use the clear to interpret the obscure.

Augustine believed that the Bible was the inspired word of God, but he was not a fundamentalist. He was never satisfied with just a literal reading of scripture in that he saw the words of scripture as signs pointing beyond themselves to the reality of God's nature or God's will for God's people.

Hymn

O God, creation's secret force,
Thyself unmoved, all motion's source,
You, from the morn till evening's ray
Through all its changes guide the day:

Grant us, when this short life is past,
The glorious evening that shall last;
That, by a holy death attained,
Eternal glory may be gained.

Almighty Father, hear our cry
Through Jesus Christ, our Lord most High,
Whom, with the Spirit we adore
For ever and for evermore.

Ambrose of Milan (340-397)
1982 Episcopal Hymnal, #14,15

Chapter Nineteen

Maintaining Hope

Terry Waite

Walking down Creed Lane in London from Amen Court and St. Paul's Cathedral to the Blackfriars tube station, a voice from within a local pub cried out, "There goes Terry Waite."

A chubby figure in a three-piece suit appeared at the door of the "public house," otherwise known as a pub. He was holding a pint of ale in one hand and motioning with the other. "Hey Terry, Terry Waite, come have one with us."

Terry looked somewhat embarrassed as he flashed his familiar bearded grin and waved back, "Some other time. I've got to catch a train."

In the almost seven years since his release from captivity, Terry Waite remains one of the most instantly recognizable persons in the world. Dubbed by the press as the "Anglican Henry Kissinger," he appeared on the world scene almost by accident.

The first time I met Terry Waite, he wasn't Terry Waite-at least he wasn't the instantly recognizable world figure whose efforts to rescue hostages would be rewarded with 1,763 days as a hostage himself.

In 1982 my son Andrew and I went to Lambeth Palace in London to interview the new Archbishop of Canterbury, the Most Rev. Robert Runcie. Terry was then the Archbishop's assistant for inter-Anglican affairs. His appointment had been something of a surprise. Terry was a layman, not a clergyman. He came from rather humble origins -none of that old school Athenaeum Club connection. Terry was a captain in the

Church Army. The first thing that struck me about Terry was his height—some six foot seven inches. There was something of a problem. The Archbishop's schedule was changed at the last minute. He couldn't give me the promised interview. Terry was joined by the Archbishop's chaplain, Richard Chartres, who is now the Bishop of London. Perhaps my son and I would enjoy a private tour of Lambeth Palace? We could take some pictures, do a feature, see the portrait of Archbishop Thomas Cranmer? Visit the Cranmer bedroom? Then Terry had another thought.

Archbishop Runcie was going to a closed-door luncheon at the BBC. Maybe they could sneak us in the back door. We'd have to be quiet and not take any pictures. The Archbishop would be briefing the news department on his just completed trip to the Peoples' Republic of China. Andrew, the editor of his high school newspaper, and I were in a state of euphoria.

There were other encounters across the years and when Terry became a hostage in Beirut, my congregation along with thousands of others around the world prayed constantly for his release. When I was in London during the time of his captivity, I even participated one day with the Archbishop's staff in the Lambeth Palace Chapel as they offered their daily prayers for his return.

As the Archbishop's assistant in the early 1980's, Terry's knowledge of the Middle East and the high quality of his diplomatic skills became apparent as he quietly negotiated the release of British hostages in Libya and Iran. When in the mid eighties he negotiated the release of Presbyterian minister Benjamin Weir and Roman Catholic priest Fr. Lawrence Jenco media attention became intense. His last mission to Beirut on behalf of American journalists Terry Anderson and Thomas Sutherland was his downfall and the liberator became a hostage himself. When he returned to freedom in 1991, he was given an appointment as "a Fellow Commoner in Residence" at Trinity Hall, Cambridge, where he committed to paper the narrative he had composed in his head. That narrative, *Taken in Trust*, was published in 1993. In it he wove a tapestry of early childhood memories along with the daily pain of isolation and captivity. He wrote out the entire manuscript in long-hand. The hardback edition sold over half a million copies in the UK alone and the paperback was distributed throughout the world.

As Terry and I sat across a kitchen table at Six Amen Court in the cathedral close, with tape recorder purring and coffee flowing, the first thing that struck me was that he was essentially the same man who had been my gracious host and guide at Lambeth Palace some sixteen years before. He remained a compassionate human person, uncorroded by the oxygen of world wide publicity. The purpose of our meeting was to understand Terry's spiritual development and how it sustained him. "Terry," I asked, " How did you become a Christian?"

Like many of the people in this book, Terry became a Christian when he was baptized. He was the son of a policeman, "Constable # 556 of the Cheshire Constabulary." Along with the position came a roomy house with a garden which produced potatoes, raspberries, cabbages, brussel sprouts, and once yielded an old George III pence. Some of his earliest childhood memories are of All Saints, Hollin Lane, Styal, seven miles south of Manchester. It was known locally as the "Tin Cathedral" He recalls the smell of pine polish and old hymn books. When he was old enough he delivered The Manchester Evening News, eventually earning enough money to buy a bicycle. At All Saints he received the basics of a Christian education, "almost by osmosis." Without realizing it he committed most of *The Book of Common Prayer* to memory and became thoroughly familiar with both the words and music of hymns, chants and anthems of the church. Before moving to Thelwall at age thirteen, he was confirmed, although he remembers little of the event except that confirmation classes were held in a room over a bicycle repair shop which contained a real elephant's leg which was used to store umbrellas and canes. He attended the local equivalent of high school, where he came under the influence of two strong, but somewhat conflicting approaches to spiritual development. Kenneth Greenwood, his head-master, took the evangelical approach, while Arthur Warburton, a "high Anglican" layreader was more sacramental and developmental. Headmaster Greenwood, "tall, lean, and fit," preached a vigorous Gospel message which called the students to make a "decision to follow Christ." Warburton, the physical opposite with a heart condition to boot, acknowledged the necessity for commitment, but was more com-fortable with "gradual growth through truth, through the sacraments." Terry acknowledged a debt to both men, "Greenwood's sheer dynamism and excitement was appealing and touched one side of my nature, whereas Warburton was able to speak to my more reflective side."

Not surprisingly, it was Greenwood who took his students to hear an American evangelist preach. Terry responded to the altar call. "I felt acutely uncomfortable; guilty for reasons I could not understand. The simple act of standing would remove the guilt and a new life would begin, the preacher said. Along with several others, I stood. I felt con-spicuous and not a little foolish. Absolute certainty did not flood in, nor has it since."

In Terry's spiritual journey he came to see the Christian faith as a "set of symbols through which I have been able to make interpretations, which in turn have helped me to find meaning in life." The church's prayer book and liturgy have tended to play a greater role in his life for, "within it symbolic life is writ large…liturgy centers around a profound mystery, which can never be explained. Now the mystery within me links with the mystery beyond and for a moment I experience a deep peace and stillness."

The religious formation of his youth and the tensions between evan-gelical and catholic traditions within his spirit were reflected in the way in which coped with his captivity. Trying to understand where his cap-tors were coming from also enabled him to ward off the "cancer of bit-terness." Daily physical exercise helped. Composing *Taken in Trust* in his head was another creative activity. So was *The Book of Common Prayer* which he had committed to memory. He recalls that he would begin each day reciting the Holy Communion service from the 1662 prayer book, setting aside a morsel of bread from his meager rations to be "the body of our Lord Jesus Christ which was given for thee." And then there were the hymns he had learned as a choirboy at school assembly and in the Church Army training program. He would hum them, sing them, chant them and savor their message of hope.

In the written account of his captivity, he made the statement, "There is not a lot of faith in me." Over coffee, he explained that his comment had to do with feeling vs. fact. "In captivity, I didn't feel the close presence of God. I felt alone, but that did not mean for one moment that I ceased to be believe. I do believe! There's a lot of nonsense about faith…the great thing about faith is that it doesn't necessarily mean that you will feel good, or feel the presence of God. It does mean that you will be able to maintain hope."

A friend once told Terry that in seeking the liberation of hostages, he was also seeking his own liberation. He pleaded guilty to the charge and went on to explain that in captivity he discovered that, "true liberation comes from the center of yourself." Terry discovered that center when he realized that his captors could hold or destroy him physically, "but there's a part of me that can not be taken from me because it's in the hands of God."

He ended our conversation in the same way he ended his book, by reciting the words that were scribbled on a cell wall in a Nazi concentration camp. "I believe in the sun when it is not shining. I believe in love when feeling it not. I believe in God even if he is silent."

Scripture

I will lift up my eyes to the hills;
from where is my help to come?
My help comes from the Lord,

the maker of heaven and earth.
He will not let your foot be moved
and he who watches over you will not fall asleep.
Behold he who keeps watch over Israel
shall neither slumber nor sleep;
The Lord himself watches over you;
the Lord is your shade at your right hand,
So that the sun shall not strike you by day,
nor the moon by night.
The lord shall preserve you from all evil;
it is he who shall keep you safe.
The Lord shall watch over your going out and
your coming in,
from this time forth for evermore.

Psalm 121
1979 Book of Common Prayer

Reflection

When I first asked Terry for his favorite scripture, he wrote," Dare you print Isaiah 28:20?" I looked it up and it read," For the bed is too short to stretch oneself on it, and the covering to narrow to wrap oneself in it." I E-mailed him back, saying, " That's not exactly the Holy Comforter, is it?" He retorted, "No, but it reminds me of the past." Then he added, "How about the first verse of Psalm 121-a psalm I also remember in dark days. 'I will lift up my eyes unto the hills ....'"

About the time I entered seminary, memory work was removed from most Sunday School curricula. The theory was that we would only remember that which was relevant to our present circumstances. Why learn by rote a bunch of meaningless phrases. Don't give out a lot of answers before the student asks the appropriate questions. It sounded reasonable and so prizes were no longer given for memorizing the 23rd Psalm, the Lord's Prayer, Ten Commandments, Apostles' Creed, Golden Rule etc. I believe we lost something. Terry Waite's "memory bank" was a wonderful treasure chest of hope. Terry's experience gives new meaning to the ancient Psalmist's declaration, "Your word is a lamp to my feet."

The researchers for the children's TV program "Sesame Street" discovered that children under three could repeat verbatim entire TV commercials and would recognize and reach for the advertised products on the shelf of the super market. This led to a whole new way of teaching the alphabet etc. Maybe now is the time to revisit the value of Scripture and the spiritual development of our children.

Hymn

> *O God our help in ages past,*
> *our hope for years to come,*
> *our shelter from the stormy blast,*
> *and our eternal home;*
>
> *Under the shadow of thy throne*
> *thy saints have dwelt secure;*
> *sufficient is thine arm alone,*
> *and our defense is sure.*
>
> *Before the hills in order stood,*
> *or earth received her frame,*
> *from everlasting thou art God,*
> *to endless years the same.*
>
> *A thousand ages in thy sight*
> *are like an evening gone;*

short as the watch that ends the night
…before the rising sun.

Time like an ever-rolling stream,
bears all its sons away;
They fly forgotten, as a dream
dies at the opening day.

O God, our help in ages past,
our hope for years to come,
be thou our guide while troubles last,
and our eternal home.

Isaac Watts (1674-1748)
1982 Episcopal Hymnal, #680

Chapter Twenty

Please Don't Come Back!

John, Charles and Susanna Wesley

The thirty-five-year-old cleric sat quietly and inconspicuously in the shadow of one of the great pillars of St. Paul's Cathedral in the City of London as the choir chanted the familiar canticles of Evensong. It's not easy to be a failure at thirty-five.

"For mine eyes have seen thy salvation," went the *Nunc Dimittis,* Simeon's song from Luke's Gospel (2:29). And that's exactly what was troubling the young priest. He had done all the things he believed the Lord required of him, and still there was something missing. At Oxford he had led a disciplined life both academically and religiously. He and his brother Charles had formed a support group that was dubbed by their fellow students as: *The Holy Club, Bible Moths, The Methodists.* Their discipline included prayer and Bible study, the weekly reception of Holy Communion (at a time when 4 times a year was the norm in the Church of England), benevolent activity among the poor, and visits to local prisons. He later reflected in his journal that he hoped to be saved by: "1. Not being so bad as other people; 2. Having still a kindness for religion; and, 3. Reading the Bible, going to church, and saying my prayers." While he sensed that something was still missing and while he prayed for "inner holiness" he concluded that, "doing so much and living so good a life, I doubted not but I was a good Christian."

Feeling compelled to do good things for God and intrigued by tales of "savages" eager to hear the Gospel, John and his brother Charles set sail for General Oglethorpe's colony in Georgia where they would be missionaries in Savannah and Fort Frederica on St. Simon's Island. Charles' position as secretary to General Oglethorpe did not work out, his health was broken, and he returned to London fourteen months after he had left. John was not far behind. His demand for rigid discipline and his insistence on re-baptizing Calvinists and Lutherans rendered him ineffective as pastor and priest to the pioneer village. Following the rejected courtship of a local lady, he was asked to leave Christ Church, Savannah.

Actually it was worse than that. John's petulant behavior brought an indictment from the local grand jury and he was deported. When he returned to England, his commission was revoked by the Board of Trustees of the Georgia Colony, who thought him strange and eccentric and "an incendiary of the people against the magistrates." Reflecting on his American experience he noted in his *Journal*, " I went to America to convert the Indians; but oh! who shall convert me? He describes himself as having a "fair summer religion ….. but death look me in the face and my spirit is troubled."

The one redeeming feature of the Wesleys' American experience was their shipboard encounter with a group of German Moravians. During the crossing John Wesley had busied himself with pastoral and educational duties, which were interrupted by frequent bouts with the elements. "The sound of the sea breaking over and against the sides of the ship, I could compare to large cannon …the rebounding, startling, quivering motion of the ship much resembled what is said of earthquakes." During a prayer service with the Moravians, he reported that "a great wave had broken over the ship, splitting the mainsail. The ship rocked and water streamed through the cracks in the deck onto the people below." A terrible screaming began among the English. The Germans calmly sang on. Wesley asked the Moravians if they had been afraid. The answer was, "No." What about their women and children? "No, our women and children are not afraid to die," was the calm matter of fact Moravian answer. They had something the Wesleys wanted but had not found. What was John looking for? "A sure trust and confidence in God, that, through the merits of Christ, my sins are forgiven, and I reconciled to the favor of God," he wrote.

It is not surprising that John Wesley sought out the Moravians in the person of Peter Bohler when he returned to England. At this point his failure in Georgia was being compounded by a string of rejections in London churches. His *Journal* was littered with notations similar to this entry of February 4,1738, "I was desired to speak at St. John the Evangelist's… many of the best in the parish were so offended, that I was not to preach there any more." Wesley wanted to quit preaching altogether, but Bohler advised him to "Preach faith till you have it; and then because you have it, you will preach faith." So John kept on—with mixed results. On March 27 he visited a condemned man in prison, who after listening, reported somewhat to Wesley's surprise, "I am now ready to die. I know Christ has taken away my sins and there is no more condemnation in me." Nevertheless, when he once again preached in two London Churches he was informed that "I was not to preach any more in either of those churches."

On his return to England, John also discovered that the health of his brother Charles had continued to deteriorate and he was in fact reported to be dying. Bohler had also made contact with Charles and visited him on what both men thought to be his deathbed. Bohler, after praying for Charles' recovery, asked him if he hoped to be "saved, and if so on what basis." Charles believed that he would be saved because "He used his best endeavors to serve God." The two men were not in agreement. Bohler said a final prayer and departed on a missionary voyage to North Carolina. It would be years before he would know how his words had affected both Charles and his brother John.

Charles' sick bed was in the home of John Bray on a street known as Little Britain, not far from St. Paul's Cathedral and just a few doors from St. Botolph's Church, Aldersgate, where the elder Samuel Wesley had served at the beginning of his ministry in 1688. Bray, a humble mechanic, took Bohler's place as Charles' mentor. To Bray, Charles confessed his "unbelief and want of forgiveness." Another friend, William Holland, brought him a copy of Martin Luther's *Commentary on Galatians*. From this Charles rediscovered what he later acknowledged could be found in the Thirty-nine Articles in *The Book of Common Prayer*, as well as in scripture and the early church fathers. "Salvation is by faith alone, not an idle, dead faith, but a faith which works by love, and is necessarily productive of all good works and all holiness." He reported that having made that discovery, "I slept in peace."

One more character needs to be added to the drama of Charles' conversion and physical recovery. On Sunday, May 21, the Feast of Pentecost, Charles was awakened by a voice that cried out, "In the Name of Jesus of Nazareth, arise and believe, and thou shalt be healed of all thy infirmities." The voice was that of Bray's sister, but Charles was convinced that they were the words of Christ himself. In joy, Charles turned to the Bible. One of the verses that came to his attention was from Psalm 40, "He hath put a new song in my mouth." Two days later Charles would write the first of the 7,000 hymns which would become his most lasting contribution to the whole Christian family.

In the meantime, John Wesley, struggling with his own faith, awakened on Wednesday morning, May 24, at daybreak. "It was five this morning, that I opened my Testament on those words, 'there are given unto us exceeding great and precious promises, even that ye should be partakers of the divine nature.'" (2 Peter 1:4) It expressed an old idea that became popular among Eastern Orthodox Christians. Irenaeus capsulated it in his famous, "He became what we are in order that we might become what he is." John, it should be noted, was a practitioner of the now questionable practice of opening his Bible at random for guidance and inspiration. One of my professors used to call this "playing Bible roulette." However, later in the day, he came across "Thou art not far from the kingdom of God." (Mark 12:34) That evening he attended Evensong in Sir Christopher Wren's recently completed architectural masterpiece, St. Paul's Cathedral.

In addition to the psalms and canticles from the Prayer Book, John noted in his *Journal*, "The anthem was 'Out of the deep have I called upon Thee therefore shalt Thou be feared. O Israel trust in the Lord: for with the Lord there is mercy, and with him is plenteous redemption. And He shall redeem Israel from all his sins."

From St. Paul's Cathedral he walked the short distance to Aldersgate Street. He says that he went to the meeting "unwillingly." The leader was reading from Luther's preface to *The Epistle to The Romans* when, "about a quarter before nine, while he (Luther) was describing the change which God works in the heart through faith in Christ, I felt my heart strangely warmed. I felt I did trust in Christ, Christ alone for salvation and an assurance was given me that He had taken away *my* sins, even *mine* and saved me from the law of sin and death."

Following the meeting, a happy gaggle of believers took John to see his brother Charles. They marched through Little Britain singing Charles' first hymn:

> *Where shall my wondering soul begin?*
> *Outcasts of men to you I call,*
> *Harlots and publicans and thieves!*
> *He spreads his arms to embrace you all;*
> *Sinners alone his grace receives:*
> *No need of him the righteous have;*
> *He came the lost to seek and save.*
> *For you the Prince of Glory died.*
> *Believe, and all your guilt's forgiven;*
> *Only believe-and yours is heaven.*

Scholars have noted that John's heart was "warmed" not "set on fire." His first inclination was to pray for those who had "despitefully used me and persecuted me." No doubt the list included all those London churchwardens who had told him not to come back.

On the following evening John returned to Evensong at St. Paul's. He received confirmation of his experience through the anthem which contained the words, "My song shall always be of the loving-kindness of the Lord: with my mouth will I ever be showing forth Thy truth from one generation to another."

But something else happened that is fairly common following an intense spiritual experience. Some call it doubt, others say it's spiritual warfare. John reported, "But it was not long before the enemy suggested, 'This can not be faith; for where is the joy?'" John's spiritual dilemma was a classic one: the attempt to define the relationship of faith and feeling. It was an especially crucial in John Wesley's case since he had convinced himself, and preached to others, that the feeling of joy was necessary to salvation. Wiser souls counseled him that "God sometimes giveth, sometimes witholdeth (joy)." It was a year later, preaching in a field outside of Bristol to a gathering of 3,000, that he experienced the joy he so earnestly desired.

Significantly, the text was the one Jesus used from Isaiah when he spoke at the synagogue in Nazareth: "The Spirit of the Lord is upon me because he hath anointed me to preach the Gospel to the poor." (Luke 4:18) The Bristol and Aldersgate experiences significantly defined what John Wesley would be about for the next fifty years.

It is impossible to write about John and Charles Wesley without including their mother, Susanna. Baptized Susanna Annesley, the daughter of a clergyman, it was quite natural for her to accept the proposal of the Reverend Samuel Wesley, the son of a clergyman. Today they would be called PKs or Preacher's Kids. They were married on November 12, 1688, and set up housekeeping in the curate's quarters at St. Botolph's, Aldersgate, just a short walk from London's still unfinished St. Paul's Cathedral. Nine years and seven pregnancies later, the

Wesleys had moved to Epworth, where they would live for the rest of Samuel's life.

In all Susanna raised ten children to maturity and buried at least four more, presided over the vicarage, conducted morning and evening devotions, and provided what we would call "home schooling" for the children six hours a day. She called it the "Little Academy." In the eighteenth century it was the norm. So was strict discipline. Her philosophy of education certainly wouldn't measure up to today's standards, in fact it would probably have gotten her in trouble with the authorities. She believed that the conquering of the will was the foundation of good child development. She counted as cruel those parents who "permit their children to get habits which they know must be afterwards broken." When her children were disciplined, they were to "cry quietly." No temper tantrums, please! Her own personal discipline included an hour a day by herself in her room from five till six for prayer and Bible reading. No interruptions, please! She kept a journal of her meditations and once noted, "Help me Lord, to remember that religion is not to be confined to the Church or closet, nor exercised only in prayer and meditation, but that everywhere I am in Thy Presence. So may my every word and action have a moral content."

She is often referred to as the "Mother of Methodism" since she, quite by chance, established the model for the Methodist class meeting. When her husband, Samuel, left the parish in the hands of the curate while he was on an extended trip to London, things fell apart and Sunday attendance plummeted. Quite innocently, what began as a household gathering of children and servants in the kitchen on Sunday evenings for prayer, Bible reading, and instruction, took the place of Sunday morning worship. Neighbors asked if they could listen in and soon there were as many as 200 at the rectory and no one in church for Matins on Sunday morning. The curate wrote to the rector and Samuel wrote Susanna instructing her to cease and desist. Her reply provides us with a window into her character. She wrote back, "If you do, after all, think fit to dissolve this assembly, do not tell me that you desire me to do it, for that will not satisfy my conscience, but send me your positive command, in such full and express terms as may absolve me from all guilt and punishment, for neglecting this opportunity of doing good, when you and I shall appear before the great and awful tribunal of our Lord Jesus Christ." The Reverend Mr. Samuel Wesley, Sr., rector of Epworth, let the matter drop.

Despite their well-documented affection for each other, the strong wills of Susanna and Samuel once clashed over political matters. One evening Samuel noted that his wife did not say "Amen" to the prayers for King William. (In 1688, in what was known as the Bloodless Revolution, William of Orange and his wife Mary Stuart ascended to the throne of England replacing James II). When questioned, Susanna admitted to Jacobite sympathies. Samuel declared that under those circumstances they could not share the same bed and he took off for London. How they eventually resolved their differences remains undocumented, but the issue of their reunion was John Wesley and, a few years later, Charles. When John was six and Charles was three, the rectory at Epworth was destroyed by fire. John in recalling the event often referred to himself as a "brand plucked from the burning."

Susanna became a widow in 1735 and to the loss of Samuel was added the plight of the penniless widow. There was no pension fund. The rectory at Epworth belonged to the church. She spent her remaining seven years living with her children. As we have already noted, the conversion experiences of Charles and John occurred in 1738. For five years Susanna supported, but did not always agree with, the "methods" of her Methodist sons. She questioned the propriety of field preaching, although John argued that the Sermon on the Mount provided a very strong precedent. She held strong High Church views on the real presence of Christ in the sacrament and questioned the idea of instant conversion. But, John recorded in his *Journal*:

I talked largely with my mother, who told me that, till a short time since, she had scarce heard such a thing mentioned as the having forgiveness of sins now, or God's spirit bearing witness with our spirit; much less did she imagine that this was the common privilege of all true believers. "Therefore," she said, " I never dirst ask for it myself. But two or three weeks ago, while my son Hall was pronouncing those words in delivering the cup to me, 'the blood of our Lord Jesus Christ, which was given for thee', the words struck through my heart, and I knew God for Christ's sake had forgiven me all my sins.

John was convinced that his mother, strict disciplinarian though she was, also knew the joy of being a Christian.

Susanna had asked her sons to sing a psalm of praise at her bedside when she breathed her last breath. This they did with tears streaming down their faces, "They cried to the Lord in their trouble and he brought them out of their distress. He stilled the storm to a whisper. They were glad when it grew calm and he guided them to their desired haven." (Psalm 107:28)

Scripture

May grace and peace be yours in abundance in the knowledge of God and of Jesus our Lord, His divine power has given us everything needed for life and godliness, through the knowledge of him who called us by his own glory and goodness. Thus he has given us, through these things, his precious and very great promises, so that through them you may escape from the corruption that is in the world because of lust, and may become participants in the divine nature.

2 Peter 1:2-4
NRSV

Reflection

As I noted in Chapter One, there is a statue of John Wesley on the north side of St. Paul's Cathedral. You have to look for it. It's off to one side in the bushes by itself. I'm told it will eventually be placed in a more prominent place when the area around the Cathedral is cleared of the now redundant buildings that sprang up after World War II. But no one is quite sure just where that "proper place" will be. How symbolic! Two hundred and fifty years after the ministry of the Wesley's, the Anglican Church is still a bit uncomfortable with those whose message and ministry doesn't quite fit in.

Like John Wesley, I have attended Evensong at St. Paul's many times. One Sunday afternoon, while walking from Amen Court to the Cathedral, I stopped to talk to a group of energetic young people who had set up shop on the plaza in front of the church. They had banners, a card table covered with tracts, and accompanied by guitars, they were merrily singing contemporary Christian songs.

"Tell me who you are and what you're doing," I inquired.

"We're from the London City Mission and we're here to tell people about Jesus."

"That's wonderful," I said. "That's why I'm going into the Cathedral."

"Well," said the perky spokesperson for the group, "If you don't find him in there, stop by on your way out!"

God seems to insist that his message be taken to the "highways and byways," and when the institutional church can't do it, he calls a St. Francis, a Wesley, a General Booth, or a bunch of kids from the London City Mission.

John Wesley's story is in many ways similar to that of Martin Luther, who we will meet in the next chapter. Both men tried to find peace and joy by keeping the rules and discovered that God's grace is not something you earn or merit, but that it is a free gift to be received and enjoyed.

Someone described the church of the Wesley's' day as the "Bland leading the bland." When John met the Moravians he knew that there had to be more to it than that. He was a restless soul and would not rest until he found the peace and joy that he observed they had.

Maybe the message we need to deliver to a restless world is that "There is more, much, much more!"

Hymn

O for a thousand tongues to sing
My dear redeemer's praise,
The glories of my God and King,
The triumphs of his grace!

My gracious master and my God,
Assist me to proclaim.
And spread through all the earth abroad,
The honors of thy name.

Jesus, the name that charms our fears,
That bids our sorrows cease;
'Tis music in the sinners ears,
'Tis life and health and peace.

He speaks; and listening to his voice,
New life the dead receive,
The mournful broken hearts rejoice,
The humble poor believe.

Hear him ye deaf; ye voiceless ones ,
your loosened tongues employ;
Ye blind, behold, your savior comes;

and leap ye lame for joy!

Glory to God and praise and love
 Be now and ever given,
By saints below and saints above,
The church in earth and heaven.

Charles Wesley (1707-1788)
1982 Episcopal Hymnal, #493

Chapter Twenty One

A New Idea On The Internet

Martin Luther

The year 1517 is one of those dates you have to remember like 1066 and 1492. They mark the end of something old and the beginning of something new. For the history student, they are convenient pegs on which to hang pieces of information. 1066 is of course the date of the Norman invasion of England. And we all remember, "Columbus sailed the ocean blue in fourteen hundred ninety two." 1517 marks the beginning of the Protestant Reformation. Actually the Reformation had been building up steam for more than a century, but October 31, 1517, was the day or rather night when Martin Luther nailed his 95 Theses on the door of All Saints Castle Church, Wittenberg, Germany. As my university history professor liked to point out, "When Dr. Martin Luther pounded those nails, he had no idea he was starting the Reformation." An unidentified voice from the back of the class blurted out, "What did he think he was doing, going trick or treat?" The professor had obviously heard that one before and without even a flicker of irritation continued, "What Luther was doing was posting an invitation to the academic community to gather for a discussion and/or debate on some current issues of general concern. The Pope had a building program underway and his fundraising committee had come up with a neat way to generate funds."

Were that professor making his presentation today, he might have suggested that Luther was simply posting a new idea on the Internet hoping that the chat room would run with it.

However, the issues that Luther raised in reflecting on the sale of indulgences cut so deeply into the marrow of what it means to be a Christian, that the end result changed the face of Christianity and Christendom for centuries to come. Luther, somewhat reluctantly, became a major vehicle for that RE-formation.

Like Jacob in the dry riverbed of Jabbok, (Genesis 32:22ff) Luther wrestled and struggled for eternal meaning and divine blessing. What came out on the world stage had first been acted out in his own life. Luther, as both his biographers and critics are fond of pointing out, was an all too human vehicle for the rethinking of the Gospel message. Paul's phrase about having this treasure in earthen vessels, comes to mind (2Corinthians 4:7). Luther indeed had both physical and psychological problems.

Back in the 1973 there was a very noble attempt to bring serious theater to the movie screens of America called the American Film Theater. The format was that of the professional stage, with its limited scene changes and strong dialogue. Yes, it was projected on the screen of a local cinema, but everything else mimicked Broadway or London's West End. Tickets were sold in advance, Playbills were passed out, and there was an intermission for refreshments and commentary. Stacy Keach's' production of *Martin Luther* was one of the offerings and it leaned heavily on Martin's gastrointestinal difficulties as chronicled by Erik H. Erickson, a psychoanalyst, in his *Young Man Luther.* (Luther suffered from constipation and farted a lot.) During the intermission, a loud voice was heard in the lobby declaring, "Make's you wonder if they had had Malox, would we have had a reformation?"

Luther, a very fragile "earthen vessel," struggled not only with personal issues of the digestive tract and his own sense of self worth, but in so doing struggled with the basic questions of the creation's relationship to the creator; of humanity's relationship to God. Do we earn God's favor or is it a gift?

Luther's conversion or coming to faith can be divided into at least two parts. There was his decision to become a monk and there was his discovery of the Gospel. There never was any question about belief in a Supreme Being. Luther and all those around him believed in God. But, what kind of a God, friendly or hostile, that was the question.

On July 2, 1505, Martin Luther, a stocky 21-year-old law student, was struck or scared by lightning outside the village of Stottenheim in Saxony. With a primal scream he pleaded, "St. Anne help me." St. Anne's influence was already evident in the Luther family. She was the patron saint of miners and Hans Luther, a peasant without land, had prospered under Anne's patronage. He had worked his way out of the mines and was the owner of several foundries. Hans' success and prosperity was financing young Martin's education. Also, in the medieval hierarchy of divine influence, St. Anne was a most accessible figure. Legend had it that she was the mother of the Virgin Mary and the grandmother of Jesus. A good word from St. Anne might make its way into the very throne room of God the Father. To his cry for help, Martin added the promise, "I will become a monk." To enter a monastery not only meant the abandonment of wealth, sex, and power (with the traditional vows of poverty, chastity, and obedience), but was the recommended road to salvation. The monastic life lived properly was believed to insure preferential treatment on the Day of Judgment. Thomas Aquinas commended it and likened entering a monastery to a second baptism. Monasticism was the superhighway to saving one's soul. So after a farewell party at the law school, Martin took the "on ramp" at the local Augustinian monastery. Hans Luther was furious.

Martin was very good at what he called "monkery." But its discipline did not produce the peace that he so desperately desired. He not only followed the rigorous prayer discipline of the order, but also excelled in mortifying his own flesh. In addition to the standard regimen, he wore a hair shirt, and slept on the cold floor of his cell without a blanket. When he was ordained a priest and said his first mass, he was terrified and almost left the altar. Like Saul of Tarsus, 1,400 years before him, he strove to observe the rules, but no matter how hard he tried, Luther wasn't satisfied and was certain that the Almighty was displeased. Under the prevailing climate of opinion, salvation was something one earned or gained by doing good works. In addition, one could access the merits or surplus credit of the saints. Special acts of devotion, pilgrimages to holy places, visiting holy relics, special masses, acts of charity or contributions to the church treasury all transferred credit to one's account. This system of merit or spiritual credit came under the general heading of "indulgences." When Luther was sent to Rome on official Augustinian business, he took the time to acquire as much spiritual merit as possible. He visited the tombs of Peter and Paul, and after climbing the stairs of "Pilate's Steps" on his bare knees and repeating the Pater Noster on each step (28 of them), he uttered what may have been his first words of doubt, "Who knows whether it is so?" According to the prevailing accounting system he had earned two million years off his time in purgatory.

God's grace works in mysterious ways. Behind Luther's spiritual journey was the figure of Johann von Staupitz, his spiritual superior, his confessor, and a mystic. He understood young Luther's compulsion for perfection, wished that he would have something big to confess rather than petty imagined infractions of the law, and once exclaimed in exasperation, "God is not angry with you, you are angry with God." When Staupitz was being urged to discharge this restless monk, he prophetically stated that, "when he (Luther) finds his peace in Christ the church will gain a champion." It was Staupitz, who recommended that Luther study for a doctorate in Holy Scripture and become a lecturer on the Bible at the University of Wittenberg, which laid the foundation for Luther's second conversion. Without Staupitz's astute insights and spiritual direction, Martin would have been just one more angry, constipated monk. With the same vigor that he approached "monkery," Luther addressed the study of scripture. Psalms, Galatians, and Romans were both spiritual gold mines and land mines which shook him loose from a backpack of old assumptions and above all introduced him to the joy of the Gospel.

When his lectures took him to Psalm 22, he was startled by the opening phrase, "My God, My God, why hast thou forsaken me." The words were written by David, but they were also spoken by Christ from the Cross. Psalm 22 continued to describe the agony of the crucifixion. It spoke of abandonment, aloneness, and isolation; of nails being driven through hands and feet; of lots being cast for his garment. This was not the angry judgmental Christ sitting remotely on a rainbow, this was a suffering servant, someone who experienced the same things Luther was experiencing. Christ the judge became Christ the savior. In discovering a new view of Christ, Luther had a new understanding of a loving God who was in Christ reconciling the world to himself. While his new perception of God unfolded as his study of scripture progressed, a decisive moment occurred in 1515 in his study in a tower while sitting on the toilet. He was wrestling mentally with the paradox of God's justice and God's love when the words of Romans 1:17 suddenly made sense. "The one who is righteous will live by faith." At that moment he was relieved, mentally, spiritually, and physically. Luther later wrote that he felt himself "reborn" and "the whole of scripture took on new meaning and whereas before the 'justice of God' had filled me with hate, now it became to me inexpressibly sweet in greater love. This passage of Paul became to me a gate to heaven."

Years later when Luther was drafting the preface to the Epistle to the Romans in his German translation of the Bible, he wrote, "Faith is a living, unshakable confidence in God's grace; it is so certain that someone would die a thousand times for it. This kind of trust, in and knowledge of God's grace makes a person joyful, confident, and happy with regard to God and all creatures. This is what the Holy Spirit does by faith." *

The rest is history. Luther's request for a debate on indulgences eventually led to the condemnation of his ideas, his excommunication, and the Protestant Reformation. For our purposes it is enough to say that Luther rediscovered that God is our friend and not our enemy.

Scripture

> *For if Abraham was justified by works, he has something to boast about, but not before God. For what does the scripture say? Abraham believed God, and it was reckoned to him as righteousness.*
>
> Romans 4: 2,3
> NRSV

> *Thus the scripture was fulfilled that says, "Abraham believed God, and it was reckoned to him as righteousness," and he was called the friend of God.*
>
> James 2:23
> NRSV

Reflection

In the spiritual pilgrimage of one German monk named Martin Luther, we see a very earthy human being going from a position of seeing God as an enemy to seeing God as a friend. In many of the scripture passages relating to conversion we run across the Greek word *metanoia*, which is usually translated as *repent*. In the Middle Ages, this was often translated or understood to mean *do penance*. As we have noted above, Luther tried penance. He tried it with a vengeance and it got him nowhere. Like Paul he cried out, "Wretched man that I am, who can deliver me from the body of this death." (Romans 7:24) While the call to repentance may well be an invitation to reject a sinful and destructive life style, it also means to turn or take a new direction. It can also mean to look at things differently, to re-think; to have a change of heart or to stand in a different place. In Luther's case there was a radical shift in the context in which he understood his life. When he discovered "justification by faith through grace," he moved from seeing law and keeping the rules as the key to a healthy relationship with God to simply accepting the gift or invitation of a loving Savior to came and be God's friend.

Luther's conversion began with fear. It was indeed "a dark and stormy night," and nothing can make one more aware of one's own mortality than a thunderstorm—well maybe a tornado or a hurricane! As a former marine officer, I remember the old axiom: "There are no atheists in fox holes." Fear of the Lord may well be the beginning of wisdom, but God does not leave us there. Fear may be the beginning. But I do not believe that it is the final destination. We might want to note that John Newton's conversion began with fear on a dark and stormy night.

Luther was an earthy man. His language, even by contemporary standards, was often crude or even vulgar. We have a medieval and puritanical idea that when it comes to the things of God, only upper case Gothic will do. Having said that, I don't think I could get away with quoting Luther in the pulpit as advising us "To fart in the Devil's face." But in his rediscovery that Christ had embraced the human condition, with sacrificial love and not judgment, Luther must have understood that to mean the entirety of human functions including those of the digestive tract. Luther's great epiphany was that one could be both holy and human. This was certainly underlined by marriage to Katrina von Bora and the rediscovery of the truth found in the Song of Songs—that one could be both a holy person and a sexual person.

As I typed out the words to Luther's *Ein Feste Burg*, which is based on Psalm 46, I was struck by how much of Luther's spiritual journey is captured in its words and triumphal tune. God is not the enemy, but a "mighty fortress." Luther learned to rely not on his "own strength," but on having Christ Jesus at his side. Luther learned to do battle with evil trusting in the ultimate victory of Christ and the power of his word over evil and death. It is a triumphant finale to the journey of a frightened law student crying out to St. Anne for help.

Hymn

A mighty fortress is our God,
A bulwark never failing;
Our helper he amid the flood
Of mortal ills prevailing:
For still our ancient foe,
Doth seek to work us woe;
His craft and power are great,
And, armed with cruel hate,
On earth is not his equal.

Did we in our own strength confide,
Our striving would be losing,
Were not the right man on our side,
The man of God's own choosing:
Dost ask who that may be?
Christ Jesus it is he;
Lord Sabaoth his Name,
From age to age the same,
and he must win the battle.

And through this world, with devils filled,
Should threaten to undo us;
We will not fear, for God hath willed
His truth to triumph through us:
The prince of darkness grim,
We tremble not for him;
His rage we can endure,
For lo! his doom is sure,
One little word shall fell him.

That word above all earthly powers,
No thanks to them abideth;
The spirit and the gift are ours
Through him who with us sideth:
Let goods and kindred go,
This mortal life also;
The body they may kill:
God's truth abideth still,
His kingdom is forever.

Words: Martin Luther, 1483-1546)
1982 Episcopal Hymnal, #687

* Translated from the original German by Brother Andrew Thornton, OSB in 1983 for the St. Anselm College .Humanities Program.

Chapter Twenty Two

Shadowlands Revisited

C. S. Lewis

Living at Six Amen Court for the remainder of August gave Lynne and me an extraordinary opportunity to pursue our collective and individual interests. Lynne, a professional artist, haunted the museums and galleries. I did research at the British Library and the London Institute for Contemporary Christianity. One of us would stand in line at the half price ticket booth in Leicester Square and then we would top off our day with a show or a concert. We were like two kids at Disney World.

The Institute was located in an old redundant church, St. Peter's, Vere Street, just a few blocks off Oxford Circus. I had attended seminars there back in the 1980s when Michael Saward and I exchanged churches. As an alumnus, I was welcomed with open arms. There was a 50p charge for the use of the library and coffee or tea was another 50p. At first I practically had the place all to myself. The August program was built around the writings of C. S. Lewis and the seminar had taken off to Oxford where there was a big celebration of the 100th anniversary of Lewis' birth. My tranquil environment was shattered when 50 Lewis enthusiasts poured out of a motor coach and flooded into the nave of the old church.

There was much excitement about Lewis in general. Much of their tour had been conducted by Douglas Gresham, C. S. Lewis' stepson. This only enhanced the excitement. Douglas, wearing a cross, greeted the pilgrims and gave them the grand tour of the Lewis home, the local pub, the parish church, as well as significant sites in the University. They were impressed not only with Douglas' childhood memories, but with the deep respect and love he had for his stepfather and the influence Lewis had left on his life. I later had the opportunity to enter into conversation and correspondence with Doug, but I'm afraid I'm getting ahead of myself. Let's start with C. S. Lewis.

It happened in public houses all over England during World War II. The pub owner would approach the radio with some ceremony. Service stopped, conversations ceased; the dart board was silent. "Let's have a little quiet." The message was repeated from patron to patron. "He's turning on the wireless."

"Who's coming on? Churchill?"

"No, it's time for Lewis."

The BBC broadcasts of C. S. Lewis became something of a wartime sensation and were eventually collected in his classical introduction to the basics of the Christian faith, *Mere Christianity*. But the Oxford don, who wrote over 30 books, including the "Narnia" series for children and *The Screwtape Letters*, was not always an advocate for the faith. His intellectual pilgrimage took him first into the realm of atheism and then into a high fantasy flight with the myths of the old Nordic gods.

Born in Belfast, Ireland, in the winter of 1898, he was the second son of a solicitor and a clergyman's daughter. Being a Christian was all part of the given of his life until he went off to preparatory school in England at age 13. In a process that became typical of his spiritual journey, there was no one moment of either positive or negative conversion. His embrace of atheism had not begun when he arrived at Chartres (the name he used in his autobiographical writing for his preparatory school) and was "complete very shortly after I left."

While he put the responsibility on no one but himself, there was a dormitory matron, dearly loved by all the boys, who dabbled in theosophy, Rosicrucianism, spiritualism, and the occult. H.G. Wells introduced the young scholar to the world of comparative religion and the idea that religion in general was utterly false, but nonetheless, "a natural growth into which humanity tended to blunder." Moving right along as he grew into adolescence, he came to the conclusion that the universe was a "menacing and unfriendly place." He embraced a couplet from Lucretius:

Had God designed the world, it would not be
A world so frail and faulty as we see.

By 1913 and age fifteen he became an atheist. "Little by little, with fluctuations which I can not now trace, I became an apostate, dropping my faith with no sense of loss, but with the greatest of relief."

It would be some sixteen years later, in 1929, that he returned to a theistic understanding of God. In the interim he served in the army, was wounded in France, grew into manhood, discovered the Norse gods, the music of Wagner, and went off to Oxford, where he would become a don and a lecturer in English. All the time he confessed a deep-seated hatred of authority, "a monstrous individualism." God at that time, if there was a God, was a "transcendental interferer."

His return to Christianity, like his departure, was gradual. He reflected that, "If you want to remain an atheist, you can't be too careful about your reading." Much to his surprise he discovered the Christian writers, with whom he disagreed, to be far more interesting than the atheists, with whom he found common cause. Of lasting impact was G.K. Chesterton's *Everlasting Man*, containing an outline of history, which made sense to Lewis. He also recalls being shocked by a fellow atheist remarking that the evidence for the historicity of the Gospels was surprisingly good. "All that stuff of Frazier's (*The Golden Bough*) about the dying god. Rum thing! It almost looks as if it had happened once."

"God was closing in," wrote Lewis, but in the process he noted two elements. One, his "adversary" was not idle and kept sowing his path with doubts and arguments, and two, God had given him perfect freedom. One day he boarded a bus outside of Magdalen College and got off at the top of Headington Hill. When he got on the bus, he did not believe, when he got off, he did.

Then came the task of evaluating his life in light of his acknowledgment of a "universal Spirit." For Lewis, no stranger to introspection, this was something of a shock. "He found a zoo of lusts, a bedlam of ambitions, a nursery of fears, a harem of fondled hatreds." And so he recalled, "I gave in and admitted that God was God and knelt and prayed: perhaps that night, the most dejected and reluctant convert in all England."

Lewis would hasten to add that his conversion on the Headington bus was only a conversion to theism. His conversion to Christianity took a little more time. His newfound theism led him to attend his parish church on Sunday and the chapel services on campus during the week. Public worship was not something that had great meaning for him at that time. But it was a matter of "flying the flag," of letting his contemporaries know where he stood.

His analytical mind went to work. He sensed that the old pagan myths pointed, however dimly, to a reality beyond themselves and he came to ask, "Where if anywhere, have all the hints of paganism been fulfilled?" He reasoned that there were really only two choices: Hinduism and Christianity. It was the historical base of Christianity that brought him over. He concluded that he knew too much about historical criticism to regard the Gospels as myth. "They had not the mythical taste....But," he wrote, "if ever a myth had become fact, had become incarnated, it would be just like this. And nothing else in literature was just like this." He concluded that in Christ, "the myth became history." His movement from theism to Christianity took almost two years and in what became his own pattern of conversion, he reported, "I was driven to Whipsnade one sunny morning. When we set out I did not believe that Jesus Christ is the Son of God, and when we reached the zoo, I did."

The word that keeps recurring in Lewis' account of his conversion is "joy" and it is not surprising that the book which records what he was to call his "blessed defeat," was called *Surprised By Joy*. Little did he realize at the time that the phrase was soon to have a double meaning.

Joy Davidman Gresham was an award winning American novelist, journalist, and poet. She once shared a national award with Robert Frost. She was the daughter of a prosperous New York non-observant Jewish family. At an early age she declared her atheism and at age 23 joined the Communist Party. She worked for the leftwing newspaper, *The New Masses*. She married a divorced man, William Lindsay Gresham, who was a writer and a heavy drinker. They had two sons, David and Douglas. Except for the sale of the movie rights to Bill's best selling first novel *Nightmare Alley*, the Greshams had very little money, and what they had Bill didn't handle very well. Bill was also a womanizer. But the marriage had a brief interlude of peace following Joy's conversion in 1946.

Joy had been moving in the direction of Christianity for some time. This was not easy for a Jew whose family history was all too full of the memory of living among people called Christians who thought that Christ's will meant floggings and burnings, gentlemen's agreements, and closed universities. But she admitted to being deeply interested in Jesus without quite realizing it. She read both the Hebrew and Christian sections of the Bible and found herself quoting or paraphrasing Christ without knowing it. Even as an atheist and a Communist, the imagery of the cross and resurrection had a way of slipping into her writings.

In the midst of a domestic crisis, Joy had a religious experience that changed her life. At a moment when she realized that she was not after all the master of her fate and the captain of her soul, she recalled:

There was a Person with me in that room, directly present to my Consciousness—a Person so real that all my previous life was by mere comparison a shadow play. And I was more alive than I had ever been; it was like waking from sleep.

"The experience of God lasted no more than thirty seconds," Joy wrote. "God came in and I changed. I have been a different person since that half minute." But while Joy came away from her experience with the assurance that she was loved and accepted by God, she didn't immediately associate the experience with Christ. At first she tried to relate it to Marxism, then to Judaism but was unable to find the double elements of "conviction of sin and followed by the assistance of God's grace." Reading Francis Thompson's "The Hound of Heaven" was helpful, as were the writings of C. S. Lewis. Finally she turned to the Gospels and found the person who had been the presence in her room. "When I read the New Testament, I recognized him. He was Jesus."

Joy shared her new faith with her husband and they started attending the nearby Pleasant Plains Presbyterian Church. The whole family was baptized there—Joy, Bill, David, and Douglas were baptized. Joy's own joy in her new faith led her into correspondence with Chad Walsh, a fellow writer and an Episcopal priest who taught at Wisconsin's Beloit College. He encouraged her in reading Lewis. Soon after, Joy began writing to Lewis and in January of 1950 she received her first reply. The correspondence continued and Lewis encouraged her to use her literary skills in behalf of her newfound faith. In 1952, her marriage in shreds, she set sail for England with her two sons. The subsequent meeting with C. S. Lewis and their eventual marriage has been documented in "Shadowlands" the BBC radio drama, which became a made for TV movie, a play, and then a commercial movie staring Anthony Hopkins.

When Joy died of cancer in 1960, Lewis was left with the care of David and Douglas. We know very little about David, the eldest. But Douglas, a practicing Christian, developed a love of gardening from his mother and Lewis' gardener, and went to agricultural college. For many years he managed a farm in Tasmania and now lives in Ireland, where he pursues a non-denominational counseling and speaking ministry. Douglas wrote of his early childhood with his mother and C. S. Lewis in *Lenten Lands*, and he adds some interesting dimensions, not only to the formation of his own faith, but to the faith of his mother and stepfather as well.

The civil marriage of Joy Davidman Gresham, age 41, to C. S. Lewis on April 23, 1956 was one of "convenience." Lewis, the 58-year-old confirmed bachelor provided Joy British citizenship and the right to remain in the UK with her two sons. When Joy broke her hip and was diagnosed with terminal cancer, several things happened, some of which were not reported in the "Shadowland " movies. They represent, I believe, a powerful convergence of spiritual power that gave Joy and Lewis the opportunity to declare and enjoy their love for each other.

Douglas recalls that when he and his brother were brought to the hospital to see their mother and to be told of her cancer, he broke into tears. When he was led into her room, she was propped up on pillows; her face had that "distinctive greenish-yellow color of terminal cancer patients." The skin around her eyes was dark. The "creature that had been his mother" reached out to him and it was only by an act of the will that he accepted her embrace. Joy tried to comfort and reassured her sons that she would be all right, but Douglas sensed that she did not believe she was going to live.

Douglas and his brother separated at the hospital entrance. Each lad had to deal with this on his own. Douglas' route home took him by the churchyard of Headington Quarry's Holy Trinity Church. Douglas' report follows:

> …..*I was no longer alone. He was there. He had been all along but now he made me know it and know also that he was sharing my grief and understanding my fear. I was given the knowledge as I wandered slowly through the churchyard, gazing about me, that if I felt that I really could not live without my mother all I had to do was ask that*

she be spared. I was not nor had I ever been a religious child, but he was there and I knew it.

Douglas went into the church and prayed at the altar that his mother be permitted to live. Part of his motivation, he later explained, was due as much to his fear of being abandoned as it was for his mother's well being. He left the churchyard at peace, convinced that his mother would get well. He told no one of the experience which he later referred to as "meeting Jesus in the churchyard." Douglas was eleven.

"Jack", C. S. Lewis, much to his surprise, had fallen in love with Joy and wanted their civil marriage blessed with the sacrament of Holy Matrimony before Joy died. A formal request to the Bishop of Oxford had been denied. A clergyman friend, the Reverend Peter W. Bide, had been summoned to Joy's bedside. He had a reputation for a healing ministry and was asked to lay hands on Joy. Following the sacrament of unction, the subject of marriage came up and Bide performed the ceremony as an act of charity, although he had no authority to do so.

Soon after, the hospital, having done everything they could, Joy was taken home to die. Jack was a most attentive nurse and at one point when Joy was in great pain and the medication had not taken effect, Jack prayed that he might be permitted to bear the pain for his wife. Douglas reports, " At once, he began to experience indescribable agony in his legs and for a while mother was relieved of her pain." It was later discovered that as Joy's bones were being rebuilt, Lewis' body lost calcium and osteoporosis set in.

Whether it was a child's prayer in the church, the husband's plea at her bedside, the priest's laying on of hands, the sacrament of Holy Matrimony, the prayers of their friends, the skill of their doctors or all of the above, Joy's cancer went into remission. She recovered to the extent that she and Jack could have a marriage in every sense of the word and travel to Ireland and Greece. The reprieve lasted almost two years. It was viewed as a gift, as a miracle.

When the cancer returned to Joy's body, Douglas returned to the churchyard:

> *Again I walked the path, from the Kilns, down alongside the stone wall to the wrought iron gate. I lifted the latch and stepped once again into His presence. Again, I was told that if I really could not survive without my mother's help and support, once again I could ask and it would be granted, but deep inside where our honesty lives caged, I knew that now, at the age of fourteen, I could make it, somehow, and I also felt that to ask for the same miracle twice would be presumptuous. I looked around the churchyard at the glowing trees and the quiet sleeping stones. I said aloud, "Thy will be done," and I walked out of the churchyard and home to the empty and desolate Kilns.*

In a conversation I had with Douglas, I asked him about Lewis' influence on his spiritual development. "Jack was responsible for my spiritual formation," he said, but then hastened to add, "Jack never preached to me as a child. He never sat me down and lectured about Christian principles and things like that. His huge influence on me was growing up in the household of a man who worked as a Christian, who lived as a Christian; he practiced his Christian faith every day of his life …and watching that example has stayed with me ever since…and in a sense it was that example that led me to Christ, far more than his books did. I have read his books, but thought I was too intelligent to worry about that sort of thing. It didn't need to be applied to my life. It was not until the Holy Spirit of God decided that the time was right and that I came into a full realization of what a fool I'd been. Jack's writing played some part in that, but it was really his example."

And what about his mother? "Like Jack it was her example, but a different kind of example. It was her enormous courage in the case of extraordinary adversity. Her behavior also, but not so much as Jack's. She was never quite as successful as Jack was at living a Christian life.

She still had a bit of a temper, while Jack had himself much more under control. But then," he adds, "I think though, if she had lived as long as Jack had …she might have got to the same stage. She became a Christian, of course through reading *Mere Christianity*."

With the example and model of both his stepfather and his mother, when and how did Douglas become a Christian?

The experience of Christ in the old churchyard did not make Douglas a Christian. That did not mean that his childhood experiences did not lead to belief in God. "I believed in God and I believed in Jesus Christ and I knew who they were. But, that's not what makes one a Christian, because belief is not sufficient. Satan himself believes in God and believes in Jesus Christ. He and all his demons know and believe the truth. What makes one a Christian is the conscious willing decision to accept Jesus' sacrifice on the cross for oneself personally and the submission of one's life to the authority of Jesus Christ. Now, that's a very different thing from simply believing in him. In my life that didn't occur till much later. I knew who Jesus Christ was and I believed in Jesus, but I didn't want to submit my life to anybody's control but my own."

As often happens, Doug's deeper faith commitment came with a personal crisis. "I was forced to take a long hard look at myself," his E-mail read, "and quite frankly I was disgusted with what I found. I was living my whole life based on pride, arrogance and conceit, assuming that I could run things and that I was capable of working out for myself what was wrong and what was right and that I did not need any instruction on moral and ethical issues. Forced to eat a whole lot of humble pie, I went to Jesus and asked him to take over my life, and thank God he did."

Douglas and his wife Meredith live in Ireland where they run a Christian Conference and retreat center.

What about Meredith, does she share in Doug's faith commitment?

"Merrie became a Christian long before I did, largely as a result of listening to *Mere Christianity* on tape.

Scripture

The fruit of the spirit is love, joy, peace, patience, kindness, generosity, faithfulness, gentleness, and self control. There is no law against such things. And those who belong to Christ have crucified the flesh with its passions and desires. If we live by the spirit le us also be guided by the spirit. Let us not become conceited, or competing against one another, envying one another.

Galatians 5:22-26
NRSV

Reflection

There is definitely a chain reaction going on in the Lewis family story. Lewis wrote a book. Chad Walsh recommended the book. Joy Davidman read the book and corresponded with the author. Doug Gresham read Lewis' *Narnia* series, became Lewis' stepson, and was deeply influenced by the man. Later he fell in love with a woman who had read the book! One might conclude that the Christian Gospel, well expressed, is catching.

There's also an awful lot of grace in this story, too! I have viewed the videos of both of "Shadowland" productions, and most of the miracles have been left out. What an opportunity there is for the Christian to just tell the story of God's grace at work in our everyday lives.

Joy Davidman Lewis, in writing about her own conversion, referred to the classic poem *The Hounds of Heaven* (see p.) The idea of God as the lover courting his beloved is a recurring Biblical theme. "You did not choose me, but I chose you," (John 15:16) was the way it was expressed in John's Gospel.

What is it that the Lord is calling me to do and to be?

Hymn

Jerusalem, my happy home,
name ever dear to me,
When shall my labors have an end?
thy joys when shall I see?

When shall these eyes thy heaven built walls
and pearly gates behold?
thy bulwarks with salvation strong,
and streets of shining gold?

Apostles, martyrs, prophets, there
round my savior stand;
and all I love in Christ below
will join the glorious band.

Jerusalem, my happy home,
when shall I come to thee?
when shall my labors have an end?
thy joys when shall I see?

O Christ do thou my soul prepare
for that bright home of love;
that I may see thee and adore,
with all thy saints above.

F.B.P. c. 1600
Hymns Ancient and Modern,#187

Chapter Twenty Three

Three O'clock In The Morning

Jaleh Mac Donald

It was three o'clock in the morning; three o'clock on Christmas morning. Jaleh hadn't slept all night. She occupied a dingy one-room efficiency apartment in a London suburb. She felt like someone or something was in her room. Alone, afraid, and hurting she cried out to the darkness.

Jaleh (pronounced Jolly) hadn't always lived in London. She had grown up in relative luxury in Iran where her father was a general in the army. Like many of her countrymen, she had sought asylum in the West following the overthrow of the Shah. As a child she had grown up in a "sort of Muslim family." They observed Ramadan, the month of fasting, and she had received religious instruction in school. Until age eleven, this included reading the Koran in Arabic. Her father, the general, she recalls wasn't very religious. He believed that religion was a thing of the heart and the conscience. In fact, he hated religious people "because he believed that religion was at the root of most of his country's troubles."

In the pre-Revolutionary days, Jaleh had many friends of other faiths including: Christian, Jewish, Bahai, Zoroastrian, and Buddhist. As a college graduate and young business woman, she and her friends dressed in a Western manner. Designer clothes were in and the practice of *Purdah*, i.e. wearing the veil and being secluded, were definitely out. From her mid teens she recalls an interest in knowing who God was. She started with the concept that "God is a very old man who is eager to punish you if you are bad." The servants helped her with her Arabic and urged her to accept and observe the Muslim law. Her father approached morality more from a social point of view. As a general's daughter, she must grow up as a lady and therefore she was not to "lie, cheat, or steal." She was to be "a good person" She particularly liked the simplicity of Bahai, which boiled it all down to, "Good think, good act, and good talk." But for Jaleh it wasn't enough to be a "good girl or a lovely woman," she wanted to find something "stronger than myself and better than myself."

In 1983 she packed six suitcases and left her job as a secretary with the Iranian Airline and headed for London. At first life in the UK was good. She located a cousin, enrolled in Hammersmith College to perfect her English, found a job, and other Iranians in exile. She participated in Iranian language (Farsi) broadcasts. Six months after her arrival she moved into her own flat in Ealing, a community west of central London near the Heathrow Airport, where there was a small Iranian community and an Iranian Church. She had questions about God and she could ask them in her own language. Everything seemed to be falling into place, but all was not well with Jaleh.

One day she collapsed in the college cafeteria, was taken to Ealing Hospital, and for a year and a half had no feeling in her left side and a loss of equilibrium. She lost her job, friends, and self-confidence. Often she would hear the phone ring, but couldn't find the energy to get up and answer it. The doctors could find no reason for her condition. She sold the little bit of jewelry that she had and often went without food. She had been taught in school that Allah would punish her if she ever visited a Christian church. Maybe this was God's punishment.

On Christmas Eve, over a year after her collapse, she was alone and she was angry. In the darkness of her room in Ealing, she started to argue with God. " What kind of a God are you anyway," she cried. "You are unjust and unfair. Why have you let me go through this hell? I tried to know you through Islam and that was hopeless. I tried through other religions and nothing happened. I even went to church because you said, 'Jesus is my son and he will help you,' but instead you sent me this sickness. Now I don't even want to be alive any more and you can't stop me. I am going to kill myself and you can't do anything about it. If you are really God I want to see you; I want to talk to you. I want to know that you are really God."

It was at that point, at three o'clock on Christmas morning, that something or rather someone happened. Jaleh describes a light in the dark room that "got bigger and bigger." Jaleh called out in her native tongue, "Are you?" and received the reply, "I am."

Her first reaction was disbelief. "I don't believe it," she said. "I must touch you, but I can't touch you because my hand doesn't have any sense." She recalls a broad smile and a voice that responded, "You can touch me. I have healed you because I love you." Jaleh was convinced that it was Jesus and she began to cry and "through my tears I could not see him." She never did touch him, but there was feeling in her hand and in her left side and then sleep came quickly.

In the morning, Christmas morning, she wondered if it had all been a dream. She moved her head. It was fine. She sat down and got up quickly. She wasn't dizzy. She felt her left hand and her left side. There was feeling. It had been Jesus, she decided. He had been there at three o'clock in the morning. "He loves me."

Jaleh decided that she must find the Christians at the Iranian church. It had been almost 18 months since she had been there and she wasn't absolutely certain how to get there. She went out on to the South Ealing Road and discovered that her equilibrium was OK. She noticed a familiar face in a car. It was a woman from the church. She was parked at a side street as if waiting to pick her up and take her to the Christmas celebration. It would be some time before she had the confidence to share her story with friends in the congregation. On Christmas morning she said nothing, she simply enjoyed being there. They sang the familiar carols and then when they ended with some contemporary praise songs, she noticed that she could clap her hands. It had been a year and a half since she had been able to clap her hands. The term "happy clappy" is often used in a pejorative sense to describe some of the new trends in church music, but for Jaleh it is a reminder of her liberation from physical pain and spiritual loneliness.

She attended the Sunday services regularly and joined a Tuesday evening house group. She recalled that her physical healing was followed by another kind. "From that time he started to heal me of the things I had lost in my life, in Iran, and in the hurt that I felt. That healing started emotionally. He taught me that it is the spiritual life that is important, not the life in this world. It doesn't matter how much money I have." When she first heard a discussion of Paul's statement in Romans (5:20), "Where sin increased, grace abounded all the more," she was not all that comfortable with the idea that she was a sinner. "I was defensive at first," she said, "and offended, but as I prayed about it I started to understand it in a very gentle way that Jesus could love me a sinner and that I was able to repent in my heart and ask Jesus to take over my life. After three months she began to share her story with her friends at the Iranian church. "Did he speak to you in English or Farsi?" was one of the first questions she was asked. "Farsi," was her answer. She was also ready for baptism.

It was some time later that Jaleh, walking near the Victoria and Albert Museum, saw a sign pointing into the churchyard of Holy Trinity, Brompton. They had just started an educational program for new Christians, called the Alpha Course. It was there that she met Andrew Mac Donald, a computer programmer and her husband to be. Andrew's religious upbringing was fairly typical of his generation in the UK. He was baptized as an infant in the Church of England, but his family seldom attended church except for christenings, weddings, funerals, and the carol service at Christmas. Both Andrew and Jaleh discovered that you didn't have to be past middle age, abnormal, or grim to be a Christian. In fact they discovered their fellow Christians to be the most normal, real, and joyful people they had ever met.

Jaleh recalls a dream she had when she was between eleven and twelve. She saw herself in a colorful print dress, cleaning and polishing in a church. She told her mother about the dream. Her mother thought that it was an impossible dream. "You are a Muslim, not a Christian," her mother explained, "but you are a tidy and clean girl. That's what the dream means." A year after her Christmas morning experience, Jaleh saw a pretty dress on sale in a shop window. She bought it and when she got home she found some lace and added a few accents. She wore the dress to a Christmas party at the church. When the photographs of the party were shared a week later, "I saw the dress; it was the dress in my dream. God was working in my life even back then when I was just a young girl."

One question had been on my mind since Jaleh had repeated the simple exchange, "Are you?—I am." Before that Christmas morning in 1983, had Jaleh read the Bible? Was she aware that, Yahweh, the name God gave to Moses, (Exodus 3:14) means "I am." Or that Jesus used that term in John's Gospel as in "Before Abraham was, I am" (John 8:58). Or had she read or heard of the famous I AM passages in John's Gospel as in I am: the bread of life (John 6:35), the light of the world (John 8:12), the door (John 10:7), the Good Shepherd (John 10:11), resurrection and life (John 11:25), way, truth and life (John 11:35), and the vine (John 15:1)? No, she didn't know about any of that, but when she shared her story with her new Christian friends and they pointed out the Biblical passages, she was excited. The references, plus the healing, plus the joy that was now in her life were confirmation that something real had happened at three o'clock on that special Christmas morning.

Scripture

Again Jesus spoke to them saying, "I am the light of the world. Whoever follows me will never walk in darkness but will have the light of life."

John 8:12

NRSV

Reflection

This story fascinated me for a number of reasons. First of all, I served as the exchange Vicar at St. Mary's, Ealing, at about the same time that Jaleh's had her conversion experience. My wife Lynne and I lived at the Vicarage on South Ealing Road, within walking distance of the apartment where Jaleh was living. Michael Saward had taken on my work in Florida for six weeks and I had the delightful experience of a very vital London parish church. I was aware of the number of Iranians in the community and of the existence of an Iranian church, but that was as close as I got. Who knows what miracle the Lord may be doing next door and we're never even aware of it.

The second reason has to do with God as light. The Psalmist used the term many times as in: "Send out your light and your truth that they may lead me." (Psalm 43:3) While the experience of God as light is not an everyday commonplace experience, it happens frequently enough to be taken seriously. The numerous "near death" reports of "a being of light" is one example of this. There are others in this book. (See Joy Davidman in chapter 23,) and I can personally attest to having a similar experience while on retreat at the Trappist Monastery in Conyers, Georgia. (See chapter 26.)

The phrase from Evening Prayer and the Office of Compline: "Be our light in the darkness, O Lord," will always have a special meaning for me.

I find in Jaleh's experience of crying out from the darkness of her own life to be a source of great hope. God does not abandon us to despair. The member of Alcoholic's Anonymous talks of receiving the power to be healed as coming to that point when they realized that they were powerless to control their own lives and reached out for a higher power. So the Christian life often begins when we discover that "we have no power in ourselves to help ourselves" and are willing to turn control of our lives over to the Lord

Hymn

> *Lord, the light of your love is shining,*
> *In the midst of the darkness shining;*
> *Jesus light of the world, shine on us,*
> *Set us free by the truth you now bring us,*
> *Shine on me, shine on me.*

> *Refrain*

> *Shine, Jesus, shine,-*
> *Fill this land with the Father's glory;*
> *Blaze Spirit blaze-*
> *Set our hearts on fire.*
> *Flow, river, flow*
> *Flood the nations with grace and mercy;*
> *Send forth your word,-*
> *Lord, and let there be light.*

> *Refrain*

> *Lord, I come to your awesome presence,*
> *From the shadows into Your radiance;*
> *By the blood I may enter your brightness,*
> *Search me, try me, consume all my darkness.*

Shine on me, shine on me.

Refrain

As we gaze on your kingly brightness
So our faces display Your likeness,
Ever changing from glory to glory,
Mirrored here may our lives tell your story.
Shine on me, shine on me.

Refrain

Graham Kendrick
Copyright 1987
Makeway Music, Halisham, East Sussex,
UK BN274ZB
Used by permission

Chapter Twenty Four

Feed My Sheep

Ferdinand Mahfood

I picked up the October 4, 2000 Miami Herald and I knew it wasn't going to be a good day. The headline on page 5B declared, "Founder of Broward charity resigns amid allegations." The article continued, " The founder and president of Food For The Poor, a Deerfield Beach charity has stepped down amid allegations of sexual and financial impropriety."

I quickly rearranged my schedule, hopped in my car and headed north on Interstate 95. An hour later I was in the reception room at Food For The Poor's international headquarters. "Aid Leader quits amid scandal" read the banner headline along with a picture of Ferdinand Mahfood on the front page of the Florida section of the Sun-Sentinal.

Just a week before I had told a congregation in St. Petersburg that I had discovered Food For The Poor, while traveling to Haiti on a writing assignment. I related how I had in fact made four trips with the organization and was so impressed with their work that when I returned from England in the fall of 1998, I had signed up with their speakers' bureau to tell the FFTP story one Sunday a month.

When Lynne and I celebrated our silver wedding anniversary I gave her a Food For The Poor house in Honduras. The cost for the 12'x12' basic structure was $1,500. It's now gone up to $2,000. Lynne has always had a heart for the homeless and has been a leader in homeless ministries in Miami and Jacksonville. It seemed appropriate to honor my bride, who had given me such a wonderful home, with a house in her name in Central America. Somewhere in Honduras there is a family who lost everything in the ravages of Hurricane Mitch, living in The Lynne Libby FFTP house.

The congregation on Florida's west coast had responded with enthusiasm to my presentation and, in addition to many individual gifts had voted to raise the money to build two homes.

I waited in the lobby for Father Paul, the coordinator of the speakers bureau. There was still a portrait of Ferdinand Mahfood over the reception desk. I waited and I remembered the first time I met him. It was on a "Pilgrimage" to Guyana, the only English speaking country in South America and it was my second FFTP journey as a religious journalist.

"Ferdy"—Ferdinand Mahfood—had a glow on his face as he stood at the side of a country road in Guyana. He was excited and stammered out, "I was looking for a place to take a leak and I found God."

Behind Ferdy was a flooded rice paddy and on the edge of the rice field was a makeshift village of small huts on stilts. The huts were built of scrap lumber, plywood, cardboard, and corrugated metal. It was the kind of picturesque shanty town an artist might have chosen to sketch for a tourist gift shop in Georgetown. Unfortunately the colorful hamlet was home to some fifty or sixty people of Hindu origin.

Among the residents was an elderly couple. She was blind; he was suffering from the after effects of a stroke. She could talk, he could see, but neither could work the nearby rice fields. Their one room house was rotting out from under them and slowly sinking into the soggy mound of earth on which the village was built. The old couple subsisted on a government pension, the equivalent of ten US dollars a month. How can you live on $10 a month? You buy stale bread and eat a slice apiece in the morning and another one in the evening. Neighbors give you a fish now and then and chicken bones to make a soup. Sometimes there's enough money left over to buy tea, sometimes not.

For the old couple it was a fortunate encounter. Ferdy Mahfood was the president , CEO, and founder of the international non-profit aid organization, which operates mainly in the Caribbean and, as of 1999, has delivered more than a half billion dollars worth of goods and serv-ices. Mahfood directed his staff to replace the old couple's crumbling shanty with a basic one room shelter and to see that they and their neighbors received regular shipments of basic food commodities.

Seeing God in the face of the poor was not some sort of rehearsed public relations statement staged to impress the caravan of journalists and prospective donors who were traveling the back roads of Guyana that day. Discovering God in the face of the poor was and is at the very core of Mahfood's own spiritual life.

When I met Mahfood, I was traveling once again as a reporter for several Episcopal and Anglican periodicals. A few days before our departure from Miami, I had received a call from Ferdy. He was plan-ning to go on the Guyana trip and wanted to know if I would be willing to "say Mass" for him and about twenty fellow pilgrims. The format for each day was an extensive field trip after breakfast, with lunch on the road, and a return to our hotel in the late afternoon. On our return we would gather to reflect on the day's experience, join in a Eucharist, then have refreshments followed by dinner. My first response was to say, "I am honored, but you know I'm an Episcopal, not a Roman Catholic priest."

"I understand that, father," said Mr. Mahfood," but you are a priest aren't you?"

"Absolutely!," I replied.

"You believe in the real presence of Christ in the Eucharist, don't you?" he queried.

Again, my response was positive.

"Well then Father," continued Ferdy, "we would like to have you say Mass for us each evening when the pilgrimage gathers at the end of each day. You see the Monsignor who was going to come with us and be our chaplain can't come. We would be honored if you would say Mass." Then he went on to explain that he had made a promise to the Lord that he would attend Mass every day and if I would cooperate, he could keep his promise. In that brief telephone exchange, I had a glimpse into the man's personality. I could see why he was so effective in what he was doing. How could I refuse!

After we had all checked into our hotel in Georgetown, we gathered around a large table in the conference room. Ferdy welcomed us and opened the meeting. "We all need to get to know each other. I'm going to tell you something about my story and how the Lord led me to the ministry of Food For The Poor. Then I'll ask each one of you to share something about who you are and what you hope to discover on this trip. Then Father Libby will say Mass for us and after that we'll call the waiter in and order some refreshments."

Ferdy was born in 1938 on the island of Jamaica in what was then the British West Indies. His parents were Lebanese Roman Catholics. In the tradition of that family Ferdinand was baptized, received his first communion, was sent to parochial school, was confirmed, and attended Mass on Sunday at the local parish church. Beginning at age seven he helped out at his father's dry goods store in Kingston. He remembers being given the task of handing out large British pennies to the beggars who would gather near the entrance to Mahfood's Commercial, Ltd. Shiny pennies snatched up by outstretched hands, with a perfunctory, "Thank you, master," in return for the charity, were part of Ferdy's earliest memories. As Mahfood's dry goods store grew into a wholesale business, Ferdy learned his father's trade which prepared him and his four brothers to take the next step into the import export business. From their father, the Mahfood brothers received the gift of knowing what people needed and striking a fair bargain. Purchasing commodities at the best possible price and delivering to those who needed them was Ferdy's basic skill, which the Lord would one day put to a special use.

While Ferdy always thought of himself as a Christian, it was on a business trip in 1976 that he had a life changing experience. He remembers that while he had "come to accept Jesus Christ on an intellectual level," he felt that he was missing the emotional love for God that would allow him to commit himself, "fully to his will." His wife Patti had given him a copy of Catherine Marshall's *Something More* to read on the flight from Fort Lauderdale to Chicago.

"As I relaxed in the air," Ferdy reported, "thousands of feet up, I began to read the chapter on 'the Holy Spirit', or the Comforter as she called Him. She described how the Spirit had wrapped her in an overwhelming love after the death of her husband (the famous Peter Marshall, chaplain to the US Senate)."

"As I read about the third person of the Trinity," continued Ferdy, "he suddenly came into my life-right out of the pages of the book! At once I was overcome. My eyes flooded with tears and I found myself praying, overcome by a power I never dreamed could exist. I had always called myself a believer, but this was an awareness of God, of a divine presence, that I had never before experienced. Out of nowhere I heard a gentle whisper asking me if I would go to Mass every day for the rest of my life. Where had the question come from? I was confused. I looked around the plane and saw no one who could have addressed me. 'Are you God?' I asked in my mind. I heard nothing more. I began to deliberate the question and finally I found myself responding in the affirmative. 'Yes Lord, I will go to Mass every day for the rest of my life.'"

Well, I now knew why Mr. Mahfood, had been so insistent that there be a celebration of the Eucharist while we were in Guyana. There was still more to Ferdy's story, but time was running out and there were still sixteen of us, overwhelmed and somewhat intimidated by Ferdy's testimony. We had at least pronounced our names and told where we were from. Then I proceeded with the celebration. I don't remember what Gospel I had originally chosen for that first Eucharist, but I quickly switched to the 25th chapter of Matthew, "I was hungry and you fed me....for as much as you have done it to one of the least of these you have done it unto me."

Religiously, we were a mixed group. I was going to say "diverse," but that term has been grossly overworked of late. It occurred to me, as I was conducting the service, that Ferdy had promised to "attend" Mass daily. Nothing had been said about "receiving the sacrament." I assumed that he would simply fulfill his obligation by "hearing Mass." I was wrong. Ferdy's hands were reverently outstretched to receive "the body of Christ the bread of heaven; the blood of Christ the cup of salvation." So it was with all of us: Roman Catholics, Episcopalians, Baptists, Methodists, and Pentecostals. We were being fed and in turn would turn our attention to feeding the poor.

Ferdy's story continued to unfold as we visited a homeless shelter with a Hindu temple at one end and an Anglican chapel at the other. FFTP had supplied, cots, mattresses, blankets and rice. The first three items were US government surplus. The rice was purchased in container lots on the world market and stored in a warehouse Ferdy had built in Georgetown. It amazed all of us that the skills Mahfood had exercised as a successful businessman were now being fully utilized by God to feed the poor.

Between the flight to Chicago and the shipment of rice there was a period of several years and many separate steps. While still on the Florida-Chicago flight, Ferdy had asked, after savoring the warm experience of God's Spirit, "Lord, what do you want of me?" A simple answer came back, "Give yourself to me!"

For most of us, giving oneself to the Lord is easier said than done. Just what does it mean and how do you go about it? In reflecting on his own journey, Ferdy said that it unfolded in four stages. There was the initial invitation and commitment. Once Ferdy had said "Yes" to God and made a daily commitment to be present for Mass, his life began to change. God the Father became his "Abba," Jesus, his brother and savior, and the Holy Spirit, his close friend and guide.

At a retreat he was introduced to prayer and to the Bible. It was suggested that he begin with Psalm 26, in which he read, "And in the Lord I will trust without wavering." Realizing that he believed in the existence of God, but did not trust him, Ferdy wept. For weeks, from waking to sleeping, daylight to darkness, the verse rolled back and forth in his spirit, "And in the Lord I will trust without wavering."

"Then one day," says Ferdy, "I discovered that God had given me the gift of faith, which I now understand to be the gift of trust. This discovery of trust was very profound for me. It was so much more than just an intellectual affirmation of God's existence. It was so long in coming, yet so simple. I flat out trusted him with everything, with all of me, with my life! I was now ready to let him have my life and learn to live for him each and every day without question."

Love was the next step. God loves us with unconditional love and calls us to love him and one another in return. Ferdy understood this intellectually, but he didn't feel it. "I wanted that love," he states, "I begged him for it and instantly he answered my plea. He filled my heart right then and there with the most incredible feeling. It emanated from the center of me; from my chest and it was so intense that I felt I would explode. I knew at that moment that I was experiencing a kind of "being" with him, a closeness I never knew was possible."

Contemplative prayer was the last great discovery. Basically it involves the discipline of silence. "Be still and know that I am God," reads Psalm 46:10. He recommends the writings of Thomas Keating for those who want to explore this discipline. "I discovered," he said, "that I could find my way back to that state of 'being' with him through centering prayer." Ferdy has also become a teacher of the discipline. The year after my visit to Guyana, I accompanied Mahfood to El Salvador. When it came time to return to Miami, he said he was staying behind in order to conduct a retreat. "Imagine my being asked to teach a group of clergy how to pray!"

Ferdy would be the first to say that commitment, trust, love, and prayer did not occur in chronological order. They were intertwined like the stands of a rope or interwoven like the fibers of a tapestry.

Altogether they tugged and pulled and set his life on a completely different course.

He attended Mass every day; read his Bible; set aside time for prayer; gave money to people and organizations helping the poor. He also dedicated his business, Essex Imports, over to the Lord. "I asked Jesus to be its chairman. As a result I watched as Essex prospered."

While Ferdy was a product of the Caribbean and Essex's business was heavily involved in that area, he began to see a different Caribbean than he had known. Little by little he became aware of the extreme poverty in the region. In many places, he discovered it was only the missionaries who even cared.

"How can I help?" he asked a missionary. "We need rice," was the reply. And so it began, word got around. One missionary after another made their request and Ferdy did his best best to feed the hungry and clothe the naked.

A major turning point came in 1981. Ferdy was in Jamaica on business and was asked by a missionary to visit *Eventide*, a poorhouse for some 700 men, women, and children who were too sick or handicapped to help themselves. Up to that point he knew that poverty existed, but he, " had never experienced the wrenching horror and tragedy of seeing such real suffering face to face."

He remembers, "We drove down a narrow dusty street where sewage ran down open gutters. Families dug through garbage in search of their next meal. Children with twisted legs and young men with leprosy begged piteously when they saw our car pass. Inside the poorhouse were hundreds of men women and children, barely clothed. This wasn't poverty, this was destitution. They sat on the floor staring into space, flies buzzing around them as if they were refuse. Some were so thin I wondered how they were able to breathe. And yet I had seen these faces before. They were the faces outside my father's store so many years ago."

At *Eventide* he met Cleveland Christi, who had a rare and potentially fatal skin disease. The temperature hovered around 100, but Mr. Christi was shivering and asked for a blanket. Ferdy recalls," I looked at the face of this poor, suffering man and saw Jesus—the suffering Jesus." At prayer later that day Ferdy turned to the figure of Jesus on the cross and asked, "Jesus what can I do to remedy this severe poverty? I do not have enough money to help all these people." Then Ferdy realized the answer was right in front of him. As the CEO of a large import-export firm he had acquired the skills to ship merchandise throughout the Caribbean. He had learned how to deal with government red tape.

It was at that point that Ferdy realized that God was calling him to be a "beggar for the poor." And that was when Food For The Poor was born. That was in 1982.

But there I was in the year of our Lord 2000 sitting in the lobby of the Deerfield Beach headquarters reading the bad news of what up to a week ago had been a good news story.

Father Paul came out to greet me. "As you can imagine," he said, "we've been under something of a strain these past few days." Painfully and in an organized manner, he laid out the story. As just about everyone at Food For The Poor knew, Ferdy had waged a lifelong battle against a bipolar or manic depressive emotional disorder. The condition, which produced great creative bursts of activity, had been kept under control with medication and Ferdy's own own personal spiritual discipline of daily communion, scripture and prayer. While the management team often found him demanding and at times difficult to work with, they deferred to his idiosyncrasies in an efficient operation which by 2000 was delivering more than $100 million dollars a year worth of goods and services to the poor of the Caribbean and Central America.

Ironically it was Ferdy's insistence on a management review and internal audit which revealed his "inappropriate behavior." So Ferdinand Mahfood, the founder and creative genius behind Food For The Poor had resigned and entered a residential psychiatric program. His wife, Patti, stood by him and together they had mortgaged their home to repay the misappropriated funds. In a parting letter to his staff he wrote, " I have not recently successfully managed my illness, and some of my behavior has been unacceptable. For these behaviors I apologize and ask your forgiveness."

Shortly before he left for the hospital he told a long time colleague and friend, " If I hadn't been crazy, I never would have started Food For The Poor."

Scripture

Then the king will say to those at his right hand, "Come you that are blessed by my Father, inherit the kingdom prepared for you from the foundation of the world, for I was hungry and you gave me food, I was thirsty and you gave me something to drink, I was a stranger and you welcomed me, I was naked and you gave me clothing, I was sick and you took care of me, I was in prison and you visited me." Then the righteous will answer him, "Lord, when was it that we saw you hungry and gave you food or thirsty and gave you something to drink? And when was it that we saw you a stranger and welcomed you, or naked and gave you clothing? And when was it that we saw you sick or in prison and visited you?" And the king will answer them, "Truly I tell you, just as you did it to one of the least of these who are members of my family, you did it to me."

Matthew 25;34-40
NRSV

"Be still then and know that I am God;
I will be exalted among the nations;
I will be exalted in the earth."
The Lord of hosts is with us;
The God of Jacob is our stronghold.

Psalm 46:11,12.
1979 Book of Common Prayer

Therefore to keep me from being too elated, a thorn was given me in the flesh, a messenger of Satan to torment me, to keep me from being too elated. Three times I appealed to the Lord about this, that it would leave me, but he said to me, "My grace is sufficient for you. For my power is made perfect in weakness."

2 Corinthians 12:10
NRSV

Reflection

My first reaction to Ferdy's departure was sadness. My second was anger. Why did God let this happen? My third reaction was to drop the story from this book.

I took a long walk on the beach. I'm not sure whether it was prayer or an argument that transpired as I was sorting things out with the Lord. The end result was that I (I really want to say "We") decided to keep *Feed My Sheep* in the book. After all, we all "have this treasure in earthen vessels" (2 Corinthians 4:7) and this book contains the real stories of real people and how the Lord calls us into relationship and service. But in so doing he does not destroy our will or personality. Would that life in Christ could be written in upper case gothic! But if that were the case, we would have to drop Augustine, Luther, Wesley, most of the characters in this book as well as King David and the Apostle Simon Peter. What fragile creatures we are and yet how patient and loving God is to care about us and to work through us to accomplish his purposes.

In Ferdy's journey with the Lord, it is fascinating to see how God has used the very skills that made him a successful businessman to launch one of the most successful aid programs in the western world. As in the case of Susan Howatch (see chapter 17) God used all of the talents, gifts and skills that were already in place to open up a whole new world of service, ministry and adventure.

In the scripture selections, it seemed appropriate to select three passages rather than just one. The classic invitation from Matthew's Gospel to serve Christ in responding to the needs of the poor is balanced by the call to prayer. When I was in Haiti we visited a home for failed-to-thrive infants. It was run by the Sisters of Charity, which is Mother Theresa's group. A smiling twenty-something moon-faced sister from India took us into a room with more than a dozen cribs. All of the children were under two; many had AIDS related problems; none had a life expectancy of more than a few years. Without referring to a chart or notes, the little sister introduced us to her "children" by name. She picked up those who were awake and told us their story. "This is Jacques, we found him on a pile of garbage near the sewer in Cite Soleil. He has been with us a month and he has gained a pound. She gave Jacques a hug and returned him to his crib. One of the women in our group asked the key question, "How can you do what you do with such obvious joy when you know the outcome is so grim? "Oh," said the little sister, "We could not do this if we did not pray for three hours every day."

And then the third passage reminds us that that we all have our inner battles and weaknesses. This chapter is definitely a work in process. But, there is good news: Food For the Poor continues to grow and to serve the poor. And God isn't through with Ferdinand Mahfood, either. Thank God he isn't finished with me either. How about you?

Hymn

> *Lord, make us instruments of your peace.*
> *Where there is hatred, let us sow love;*
> *Where there is injury, pardon;*
> *Where there is discord, union;*
> *Where there is doubt, faith;*
> *Where there is despair, hope;*

Where there is darkness, light;
Where there is sadness, joy.

Grant that we may not so much seek to be consoled as to console;
To be understood as to understand;
To be loved as to love.
For it is in giving that we receive;
in pardoning that we are pardoned;
and it is in dying that we are born to eternal life. Amen

Prayer of St. Francis
1979 Book of Common Prayer

Chapter Twenty Five

She Went Home At Lunchtime

Cassie Bernall

A week before the opening of the Lambeth Conference, there was a special ceremony at Westminster Abbey to dedicate a new section set aside for the Christian martyrs of the 20th Century. Along with the notables of the past, they unveiled the figures of Martin Luther King, Jr., Dietrich Boenhoffer, Archbishop Luwum of Uganda, Archbishop Ramos of El Salvador, and many more. Had they waited a year, they might have added a space for a 17-year-old girl from the suburbs of Denver, Colorado.

When students and faculty entered Columbine High School in Littleton, Colorado, on Tuesday, April 20, 1999, it seemed like any other spring day. The dating game was in full swing, summer plans were being made and, for the seniors, college acceptances were coming in and graduation was only a month away. It was "cookie day" in the cafeteria and for many of the seniors it was weed smoking day, but for two male seniors it was also the 110th birthday of Adolph Hitler.

Most schools note the advent of Spring with the appearance of graffiti on the bathroom walls. The custodial staff is instructed to wipe it away on a regular basis. While most of the scribbles deal with matters sexual, there was on the wall that day an ominous scrawl: "Columbine will explode one day. Kill all the athletes-all jocks must die."

The suspected authors of that inscription were Eric Harris and Dylan Klebold, leaders of a group known as the "Trench Coat Mafia." They had their own web page on the Internet, their own table in the cafeteria, and when they made a strike at the bowling alley they celebrated with a hearty "Heil Hitler!" For more than a year they had been plotting the destruction of their school and as many of their fellow students as possible. In particular they hated jocks, minorities, and Christians. The garage of the Harris home became a small munitions factory.

At 11:30 a.m. the carnage began. Before high noon the swat teams had arrived and the TV helicopters droned overhead catching glimpses of terrified youth scrambling out of windows and dashing for cover across the parking lot. When it was all over,15, including the two assailants, were dead. Of the 13 victims, one was a teacher. Of the dead students, five were athletes, several were high profile Christians, and one was black. The bullets took out the school's valedictorian, future scientists, doctors, musicians, writers, and missionaries.

One victim in particular captured international attention. When the gunmen entered the library they confronted Cassie Rene Benall and demanded, "Do you believe in God?" She said she did and they shot her.

Some reports claim that she said, "There is a God and you need to follow along God's path." The assailants screamed, "There is no God!" and discharged their weapons.

Some say that she not only said that she believed in God, but that she "loved Jesus."

The coroner's report indicated that the muzzle of the shotgun touched her head and that she had raised her hand to protect herself. One of her fingers was blown off.

Valeen Schnurr also stated that she believed in God. The assailants fired at her. She received 16 wounds, and somehow, miraculously, survived. Rachael Scott, whose Christianity also annoyed the assailants, was shot down.

Then there was Isaiah Shoels, an Afro-American student. They shouted "Nigger!" as they pulled the trigger and then they cheered.

Cassie Bernall was described as a beautiful 17-year-old girl with hair like corn silk. She was a "born again" Christian who carried a Bible to school and wore a bracelet with the inscription, "What would Jesus do?" Her hair, which reached halfway down her back, would soon be cut short to make a wig for children going through chemotherapy. Her ambition was to go to medical school and become an obstetrician. The previous summer she had been to England and Scotland and she hoped to return as a student at Cambridge. Her favorite movie was *Braveheart.*

But Cassie had not always been a model student. As she entered adolescence Brad and Misti Bernall became concerned with their daughter's anger and rebellious behavior. Her parents became suspicious and searched her room. What they found horrified them. There were drawings of knives and vampires, books on Satanism, Marilyn Manson records, and a collection of letters. A "best friend" had written to Cassie about all kinds of sex, alcohol, marijuana, self mutilation, witchcraft, a satanic church, and drinking a kitten's blood. There was discussion of killing an unpopular teacher, their parents, and committing suicide. One note contained the verse:

> *Prick your finger, it is done,*
> *The moon has now eclipsed the sun.*
> *The angel of dark has spread his wings,*
> *The time has come for better things.*

Cassie once confided to a friend that she had "given her soul to Satan." She later wrote that she hated her parents and God "with the deepest, darkest hatred. There are not words that can accurately describe the blackness I felt." How far she had traveled from the picture of her at seven wearing an angel costume. One might note, parenthetically, that at 14 Cassie's life and those of her assailant were pretty much on the same track.

Her parents became pro-active. They took Cassie out of the public school and cut her off from her "friends." She was enrolled in a private Christian school. The "friends," needless to say, fought back, calling her at all hours, leaving notes, driving by the Bernall's house and yelling obscenities in the middle of the night. Cassie's parents even had to get a court order to protect themselves and their children from harassment. Then the Bernalls sold their house and moved to a new neighborhood. Misti Bernall quit her job to be closer to her daughter and later reflected, "Nothing is so grueling as giving a child your attention and time when she doesn't want it." Her father described the new regime as, "No freedom, no rights, no privileges, no trust."

Under the new order, the only place Cassie was allowed to go was the West Bolles Community Church where Brad and Misti had been married. The church had a youth group with more than 200 active members and a full time young minister, Dave McPherson. At first Cassie wore a protective shell that defied penetration. Her parents were advised "to pray for a miracle.

Cassie did not like the new order of things and she certainly did not like her new Christian school. She did, however, make one friend who invited her to spend a weekend with some friends from her church. Cassie's parents reluctantly agreed and had second thoughts when they watched the group board the busses. They were a gaggle of "Goth types, dressed like punk rockers—alternative types with weird hair."

When she got off the bus three days later, she told her mother, "I've changed!"

The group had gone to a conference center up in the Rocky Mountains near Estes Park. The theme of the weekend was overcoming the temptations of evil and breaking out of the selfish life. Cassie's friend Jamie does not remember anything that was said. She remembers that Cassie began to respond to the music at the evening praise service. Jamie described Cassie as "closed." but little by little her defenses began to crumble. "Cassie began to cry. A lot of kids were walking up to the front and placing drug paraphernalia on the altar." Cassie shared with Jamie how sorry she was about all of the things she had done and how scared she was that her brother Chris would follow in her destructive path.

Cassie later recalled that Jamie was the one person she could talk to and listen to. She was "open minded and accepting." It was Jamie who told Cassie about Christ in a "noninvasive and inoffensive manner."

Cassie did not have anything to put on the altar that night. Her parents had taken all of that stuff away, but she made a decision to "turn her life around."

After the service Cassie, Jamie, and a couple of boys went out on the edge of the mountain and looked at the stars. Jamie remembers, "We just stood there in silence for several minutes totally in awe of God. It was phenomenal; our smallness, and the bigness of the sky. The brightness of God was so real." The date was March 8, 1997.

Brad Bernall, Cassie's father, remembers a "bouncy" girl getting off the bus. "It was as if she had been in a dark room, and somebody had turned the light on." Misti was happy, but skeptical and for a long time she hesitated to let down her guard.

Cassie still carried her books in a backpack and worried about her weight, but she made no secret of her faith by carrying a Bible to school and wearing a bracelet with the inscription "What would Jesus do?" Cassie participated in a weekly Bible study and she went into the inner city with members of her youth group. Their special project was a residence for young men off the street who had a serious substance abuse problem. Cassie and her friends would share a meal, play basketball, and just hang out with the residents. When she died she was preparing for a study on the subject of peace. She told her friends, "You really can't live without Christ. It's like impossible to really have a true life without him." The day after her death her brother Chris found a poem Cassie had written about discovering what it really means "to suffer and die with him."

Now I have given up
on everything else—I have found it
to be the only way to really know
Christ and to experience the
mighty power that brought
him back to life again, and to find
out what it means to suffer and to
die with him. So, whatever it takes
I will be one who lives in the fresh
newness of life of those who are
alive from the dead.

When the memorial service for Cassie was held, the overflow congregation heard from Cassie via a video tape made only two days before her death. She spoke of discovering God's kingdom by being a good friend and a good example to non-believers as well as fellow Christians. She stated, "I'm trying not to contradict myself and to get rid of all hypocrisy and just to live for Christ."

Fellow student Jeffrey Holton captured the feelings his schoolmates with the words he composed and sang:

There beside the shining sea
Enshrouded in tranquillity,
I can almost see you.
Then someone takes you by the hand.
You look to see the loving man.
Welcome home.
You went home at lunch time.

Scripture

> *They went to Capernaum; and when the sabbath came, he entered the synagogue and taught. They were astonished at his teaching, for he taught them as one having authority; and not as the scribes. Just then there was in their synagogue a man with an unclean spirit, and he cried, what have you to do with us, Jesus of Nazareth, have you come to destroy us?*

> Mark 1:21-24
NRSV

Reflection

Nine weeks after Cassie's death, it was reported that a young man was walking around in a Littleton shopping mall dressed in an open black trench coat and wearing a T-shirt with the inscription, "We're still ahead thirteen to two."

When Columbine High School reopened in late August of 1999, all signs of the massacre had been eliminated. All the classrooms had been repainted. The students had been given pep talks about respecting fellow students who are "different." Everyone was committed to a "new day" and "moving on." But, at the end of the day a custodian reported that swastikas had been painted on the wall of one of the men's bathrooms.

Evil, it appears is always with us. But, if we believe Mark's Gospel, Jesus' ministry was about confronting evil and overcoming it. Read through Mark's Gospel and you will see Jesus coming up against all that would destroy or hurt God's children. The present generation of young people are faced with some raw forms of evil "which corrupt and destroy the creatures of God." (Baptismal office, *1979 Book of Common Prayer*, p.301)

Cassie's story bears witness to the power of Christ to overcome evil and to liberate us from its power. As I indicated in my opening reference to Westminster Abbey, Cassie deserves to take her place with the other 20th Century martyrs. Cassie's mother points out that the original meaning of the word *martyr* was not someone who had been killed. It was someone who was willing to be a witness.

According to the Rev. David McPherson, the youth minister at the West Bolles Community Church, he receives a least ten requests a week from all over the country for members of the youth group to come at tell the Columbine story. Such a group came to Ft. Lauderdale, Florida and filled the baseball stadium. The speakers told their story, declaring that, "Cassie stood up for God," and then appealed to their peers to follow her witness and "Say, yes to God"

Cassie's parents are aware of the fact that their decision to be proactive in Cassie's life and rescue her, which eventually led to allowing her to transfer to Columbine High School where she was killed. She has come to see Cassie's death, "not so much as a defeat as a victory. The pain is no less. It will always remain deep and raw. Even so, I know that her death was not a waste, but a triumph of honesty and courage. To me, Cassie's life says that it is better to die for what you believe, than to live a lie."

Amazing Grace! How sweet the sound.
That saved a wretch like me!
I once was lost but now am found,
Was blind but now I see.

Twas grace that taught my heart to fear,
And grace my fears relieved;
How precious did that grace appear
The hour I first believed!

The Lord has promised good to me,
His word my hope secures;

He will my shield and portion be,
as long as life endures.

Though many dangers toils and snares,
I have already come;
Tis grace that brought me safe thus far,
And grace will lead me home.

When we've been here ten thousand years,
Bright shining as the sun,
We've no less days to sing God's praise
Than when we've first begun

John Newton (1725-1807)
1982 Episcopal Hymnal, #671

Chapter Twenty Six

His Story-Our Story

Rediscovering Grace

"All good things come to an end," or so I was told by my Nana when we left the Christmas show at Radio City Music Hall and headed for the Long Island Railroad Station and the train ride home to Douglaston.

I will miss all of my new friends who have trusted me with their stories.

Dr. George Carey, the 103rd Archbishop of Canterbury, has said that, "the Lord never leaves the same fingerprints, twice." And one of my discoveries in writing this book is that no two stories are the same. But, nevertheless, the Lord has left his fingerprints all over the world. The 25 stories in this small volume are received as circumstantial evidence that God is alive and at work in this world, constantly calling women and men, boys and girls, into relationship with God through his son, Jesus Christ. We also find evidence that God is forever commissioning us through his Spirit to minister in a troubled and dysfunctional world.

I wish I could go on telling more stories. They are everywhere and they keep coming in.

There was Christopher Rose, a former member of the Jamaican parliament, who received an assassin's bullet and was clinically dead. His out of body experience was not a pleasant one. There was a dark lake covered with mist. There were figures in the lake and there was moaning and muffled cries.

There was Bishop Ben, The Rt. Rev. Waiohau Rui Te Haara, of the Northern Region of New Zealand. Bishop Ben's ancestors, the Maoris, are descendants of the Polynesians who migrated to the northern island of New Zealand between the ninth and fourteenth century. When the British arrived the Maoris fought valiantly for their land. Bishop Ben was born on a battlefield where the Maoris and the British made war. Part of his family story was that of his grandfather, who as an act of reconciliation found the bodies of a hundred British soldiers, who had been buried in a common grave and re-interred them in individual graves with a Christian burial. If that's what Christians were all about, reconciliation and forgiveness, then Ben wanted to be one too and carry on the tradition.

There was Melanie Bainton Campbell, a happy clergy spouse from Newport on Tay, near the famous St. Andrews Golf Course in Scotland. She teaches religion and sports in a local primary school. She has always been a Christian and never had "a crash bang wallop. Being a Christian, and knowing Jesus is a gentle knowledge I have always had."

I especially remember Juan, a young man from Latin America, who was struggling with his own sexual identity, and his desire to be a priest. Juan was listening carefully to the debates at Lambeth.

And there was Hai Joon Choung from Korea. His parents were Christians and he was baptized as a baby. At age eighteen he decided that he, "wanted to be a real Christian." He enrolled in the Anglican College in Korea and began his studies for the priesthood. When he was 24 he asked to be re-baptized. "Why?" he says, "I don't know—I mean I can't say it properly. It's just that I believe God wants us to do something and I try to follow what God says."

And back at St. Paul's Cathedral there was Lucy Winkett. She was a minor canon who looked and sounded like Mary Martin. She was the first female clergyperson on St. Paul's staff. Her coming to faith as an adult and her call to ministry took place at the same time and the same place. She had graduated from Cambridge and was headed for a career in music when she attended an Evensong service in a parish church in Buckinghamshire. "As I thought about attending the Royal Academy," she recalls, "It wasn't so much that a music career was wrong, but that being a priest was right—and at that time women couldn't be priests!"

At the time I met Lucy, the BBC was doing a documentary on St. Paul's and picked up on the fact that one of the very senior canons on the staff was opposed to the ordination of women and refused to take communion from her or be present when she was the celebrant. She was not happy with the attention she was getting. "Happiness is boring on TV," she said "The media are always looking for conflict. When there is harmony or agreement at a meeting, the cameras turn off." When the BBC documentary finally aired, the Cathedral received over 1,400 letters supporting Lucy and less than a dozen in opposition.

They all had moving stories to tell. In some cases, my notes were misplaced; in others the tape recorder malfunctioned. And in some cases, I felt that the Lord was still working on them and that setting their story in 12-point type just might freeze them into an unfortunate position. But know this for certain: God is at work in the world.

When William James wrote *Varieties of Religious Experiences* on the eve of the 20th century, he indicated that there are two kinds of people: the "once born" and the "twice born." That observation may still be valid, but within those two categories there are an infinite number of variations. My old friend Gert Behanna used to point out that she was a woman who had two sons. Both embraced the Christian faith. One was a priest and one was an alcoholic. "Bard," she said, "was a natural Christian and crossed the river of faith at it narrowest point." Bill, on the other hand, "inherited all of my weaknesses and had to hit bottom before he could turn to the Lord."

Having asked all of these people how they came to faith, it is only fair that I share a bit of my own story and how it intersected with the Lord's story.

My birth on November 1, 1930, was celebrated with my "christening" shortly thereafter at a private afternoon rite at the Cathedral of the Incarnation, Garden City, Long Island, New York. Uncle Ed, a canon of the Cathedral and my grandfather's younger brother, did the baptizing according to the then new 1928 Book of Common Prayer. All four of my grandparents were present and there was a party in Douglaston afterwards. Not surprisingly, I have no memory of this at all. I was given the name Robert Meredith Gabler Libby, which was a big handle for a little guy, but the Great Depression was settling in and my parents decided that two girls and one boy was about all they could afford. The two middle names were thrown in to please both sides of the family.

Sunday school at Zion Church followed. There was a Mrs. King who ran the children's chapel in the church basement. She was a beautiful and loving woman who knew us all by name and was always overjoyed to see us. She told us stories about Jesus. We took turns lighting the candles, carrying the cross, and taking up the collection. There was always the temptation to put an empty envelope in the plate and sneak the nickel into nearby Shapiro's Candy Store during the week. Somewhere during the grammar school years I rebelled to the point of pretending to walk to Zion Church but stopped at the Community Church Sunday school, where most of my friends were going. I was surprised at how long it took Dr. Riley and the Sunday school superintendent at Zion Episcopal Church to miss me. The family, much to their credit, tolerated my absence, but by age thirteen I was back at Zion-on-the-Hill and enrolled in confirmation class.

I don't know what I, or the other kids, expected from confirmation. Most of the instruction had to do with finding things in the Prayer Book, avoiding temptation, how to receive Holy Communion, and what to wear and what to do when Bishop DeWolfe came for Confirmation. There was a lesson about people receiving the Holy Ghost when the Apostles laid hands on them (Acts 8:14-17) and some of us were disappointed that we didn't get "spooked by the Ghost." One of my peers feigned intoxication as he received the communion wine and was yanked back to his pew by an embarrassed grandparent. The family was all there, including Aunt Ethel, my godmother, who had come down from Boston for the big event. We all went out to Sunday Dinner at Julia's Restaurant in Bayside. Everyone kept congratulating me and acting as if I had just done something important. The anthropologist Margaret Mead once referred to confirmation as a "Christian bar Mitzvah." Maybe that's what it was. I didn't think that anything had happened, but looking back over a lifetime, I believe that while "more was begun than accomplished," *something* had begun. I came away with a sense that God loved me; that he had a purpose for my life; that Holy Communion was a place where the Lord would be present for me; and that God cared about how I behaved. This last point set up all kinds of conflicts when adolescence kicked in and I discovered what girls were all about.

I also had fleeting thoughts about the ministry, but they were in fact just that, fleeting. Grandpa Gabler was a contractor and he made it through the Depression appraising fire losses and in some cases getting the contract to rebuild. From the time I was ten, I would accompany him on Saturdays, crawling over charred ruins and holding the end of a tape measure as he calculated the loss. The fathers of two of my friends were architects and I marveled at their renderings and borrowed back copies of their architectural magazines. Between high school and college, I went to work for a friend's father in New York City as an office boy and junior draftsman. I actually did some work on the Delaware Memorial Bridge, a fact I have told my children, ad nauseam, whenever we drove from Florida to Long Island.

Georgia Tech was exciting, but so was All Saints Church near the Tech Campus on West Peachtree Street. All Saints was everything Zion Church was not. At least that was the way it seemed to me at that time. Sometimes you have to go off to a far country before you can hear what the Gospel is really all about. Thoughts about the ministry began creeping back into my consciousness. Phil Smith, later Bishop Smith of New Hampshire, took a group of us to visit Virginia Seminary in Arlington, Virginia, one weekend. There was much talk about the ministry before, during, and after the trip. I began, ever so reluctantly, to picture myself in a clerical collar and I began reading the Gospels on my own.

A defining moment came in the most unlikely place. There was an architectural exhibit at Rich's Department Store in downtown Atlanta. There was a big "before and after" presentation by a group from London on the reconstruction of the city after the Blitz. One dramatic picture showed a battered St. Paul's Cathedral standing in the midst of smoke and flames. The British architects were very proud of their new "housing estates" which replaced the former colorless workers flats.

"Were there any problems with the new high rise apartments?" asked one of the students.

"We did run into one problem," stated the senior member of the firm. "The new tenants had never lived in a building with central heating and when they moved in, they filled the bath tubs with coal, even though there were neither fireplaces nor pot bellied stoves in the flats. We not only had to provide new homes, but we had to teach them a new way to live."

As simple as that experience was, I had turned a corner. New shelters are important, but could not be fully utilized or enjoyed without a "new way to live." To paraphrase C. S. Lewis, when I walked in the door of Rich's, I was going to be an architect. When I walked out, I was headed for the priesthood.

No flashing blue lights, claps of thunder, or the Alleluia Chorus for me. It was more like Andrew's response to Jesus' invitation in John's Gospel to "Come and see." (John 1:39)

Many years later, at a low point in my ordained ministry, it was my habit to begin the morning with a mug of coffee and a quite time with the Scriptures. I would read until something jumped out at me. Then I would commit the verse to memory and begin a 2-3 mile jog repeating over and over the selected verse. I had just begun Paul's Letter to the Philippians and the sixth verse caught my eye and I ran with it. "He who has begun a good work in you will bring it to completion." (Philippians

1:6) It turned over and over in my mind and then on my lips as I ran the course. I was discouraged and on the verge of quitting the ministry, but there it was, "He who has begun a good work in you will bring it to completion." I do believe that the Lord spoke to me that morning.

One other experience of God's grace comes to mind. I was on retreat at the Trappist Monastery at Conyers, Georgia. *The Forgiveness Book,* which had its beginnings at the monastery, had been published. I was at work on its successor, *Grace Happens.* I had also moved to Key Biscayne, Florida, where I had become rector of St. Christopher's by-the-Sea, and headmaster of the church's school. St. Christopher's, as it turned out, was a little too close to the sea and we were digging out and recovering from the ravages of Hurricane Andrew. I was tired, but otherwise in good spirits. At the early morning Eucharist I was sitting in the back row of the choir stalls which are reserved for retreat house guests. When I got up to go to the altar to receive Communion, I was bathed in a warm light. It reminded me of a "beam me up, Scotty" moment in television's long running "Star Trek" series. I assumed that the morning sun had broken through a window. When I returned to my bench, I looked for the source of that light. I could find no window to justify the event. I stood in wonder and fought off my tears. It had been a beautiful moment, a benediction. I went back to that seat at every service from then on, but it never happened again. It didn't have to. I had gotten the message. God was keeping his promise and I knew that, "He who had begun a good work in me would bring it to completion."

Some quick observations: I was amazed at the number of people I spoke to who went straight to the Gospels and were moved to faith by reading the four evangelists. The Bible, which had been written more than 1,900 years ago and had been filtered through many cultures and many translations, still had the power to move and change lives. I believe that it was John Coburn, Bishop of Massachusetts, who first alerted me to the idea of connecting "His Story" with my story. It's amazing how many people have been able to do just that.

I also discovered the tremendous impact of hymns to carry the message of God's love and how the meter and the music settled into an individual's subconscious to be recalled at the appropriate moment. This was especially true of Susan Howatch and Terry Waite.

"None of us lives to himself and no one dies to himself," state the old words from the Rite I Burial Office. And I want to add, no one becomes a Christian by himself, whether it be Bishop Francis of the Sudan, Eileen Carey of Lambeth, or this author. None of us would be alive, much less enjoying the Christian life, without the help and witness of someone else.

When I first considered the idea of this book, I believed that it would be mainly about bishops from around the world, which in turn would give an overview of the great expanse and diversity of the Anglican Communion. As I noted in my first chapter, it didn't turn out that way. Books have a way of taking on a life of their own. This is not a book about bishops. If anything, it's about young people. Fully two-thirds of the stories tell of youthful experiences that led to a life of faith. It's hard to forget the wild young Billy Frank Graham burning up the back roads of North Carolina or the child in occupied Hong Kong living with a bomb on the roof. And I remember a little girl in Ghana looking at the horror of the crucifixion and wondering how anyone could call the day that memorialized it, Good Friday. But this book still gives an overview of the Anglican Communion, but not in the way I had expected.

And then there are God's fingerprints all over the place and the realization expressed in John's Gospel, "You did not choose me, chose I chose you." (John 15:16) Joy Davidman Lewis identified this phenomena as did Augustine and many others. The classic religious poem, *The Hound of Heaven* by Francis Thompson, captures the idea.

> *Still with unhurrying chase,*
> *And unperturbed pace,*
> *Deliberate speed, majestic instancy,*
> *Came on the following feet*

And a voice above their beat -
Naught shelters thee, who wilt not shelter me.

On my last day in London in the summer of 1998, I attended a week-day Matins at St. Paul's Cathedral. It was in a small chapel in the north transept and there were only a few people there. A handful more would come in during the office and stay for Holy Communion. The Morning Office was not a positive experience. The two minor canons appeared to be in some kind of a race. By the time I found the proper Psalm, they were into the *Te Deum*. I tried to console myself with Susan Howatch's discovery that worship wasn't entertainment. OK, but couldn't it be a little more user friendly? I was doing a slow burn and negative thoughts about the institutional church swept over me. As we say in Miami, "It was the beginning of a bad hair day." The Eucharist followed Matins. But at some point in the celebration, I had a new thought. In spite of all the church's obvious faults and shortcomings, it had been an effective vehicle for presenting Christ to me and me to Christ.

Then I looked at the altar. It had been changed. Incorporated into the reredos was William Holman-Hunt's famous painting of Jesus standing with a lantern and knocking at a vine covered door. Legend has it that at the unveiling, a spectator said to the artist, "But Mr. Hunt, the picture is not finished. There is no handle on the door."

To which the artist is said to have replied, "It is finished. The door to the human heart is only opened from the inside."

Scripture

I am standing at the door knocking; if you hear my voice
and open the door, I will come in to you and eat with you,
and you with me.

Revelation 3:20
NRSV

Hymn

Jesus loves me this I know,
For the Bible tells me so.
Little ones to him belong;
We are weak, but he is strong,

Yes, Jesus loves me!
Yes, Jesus loves me!
Yes, Jesus loves me!
The Bible tells me so.

Jesus loves me
When I'm good,
When I do the things I should
Jesus loves me
When I'm bad,
But it makes him Oh so sad.

Refrain

0-595-16403-X

Printed in the United Kingdom
by Lightning Source UK Ltd.
9550000001B